# Rethinking Emilie Frances Davis

## Lesson Plans for Teaching Her Civil War Pocket Diaries

*Edited by Karsonya Wise Whitehead & Conra D. Gist*

Apprentice House

Baltimore, Maryland

First Edition

Printed in the United States of America

Paperback ISBN: 978-1-62720-031-8
Ebook ISBN: 978-1-62720-032-5

Design by Sara Killough
Cover art by Calvin Coleman
Edited by Ronald Harris, Jr.

Published by Apprentice House

Apprentice House
Loyola University Maryland
4501 N. Charles Street
Baltimore, MD 21210
410.617.5265 • 410.617.2198 (fax)
www.ApprenticeHouse.com
info@ApprenticeHouse.com

*For my mother, Bonnie Nix Wise,*
*who taught me (over & over again)*
*to face every struggle*
*as if victory was my only option*
*–KWW*

*To everyone who fights the good fight!*
*–CDG*

*One can write for a nameless, faceless, audience,*
*but the act of using one's voice requires a listener*
*and thus establishes a connection.*

*For African-American women the listener*
*most able to pierce the invisibility*
*created by another Black women's objectification*
*is another Black woman.*

-Patricia Hill Collins, *Black Feminist Thought*[1]

*I write; therefore, I exist and feel and, therefore, I am.*

-Karsonya Wise Whitehead, *Notes from a Colored Girl*[2]

# Contents

# Preface and Acknowledgements

When I finished my last draft for this project I immediately called my mother. I had a nagging sense of guilt that my priorities were out of order; that my attempt to honor every gift (and this project is a gift) was misguided. But she simply congratulated me and said "one down and on to the next one." My parents' consistent encouragement to step forward and pursue my passion for teaching, learning, and research is such a precious gift. My father's phone sermonettes from Texas remind me of essential truths that serve as an anchor to my soul. Steady love from a brother and sister-in-law and the precious joy beautiful baby nephews give are most certainly gifts. There are also the prayers and calls from aunties, uncles, and cousins; the carefree happiness I experience when I connect with TX, BK and Casa Whitney friends—all gifts that keep my spirit alive. I am also very grateful for faculty and leadership in my department and mentors in my doctoral program who have supported and believed in my ability to make contributions to the field of teacher education—invaluable gifts of collegiality and opportunity. If I worked backwards to thank everyone who has invested in me and inspired me I would exceed my allotted space and undoubtedly only scratch the surface. Therefore, I simply thank the goodness that finds me and gifts me with such people—the God who sovereignly bends my life towards His will. –*CDG*

\*\*\*\*\*\*

I believe in the good. I believe that good things happen to people whether they are good or not. I believe that good ideas once spoken become a part of our collective consciousness and though there are very few new ideas, there are new ways of approaching old ideas and new solutions for answering old questions. I believe that good books must start and end well so I always read the first and last chapters of a book before I commit to reading the rest of it. I believe that the most revolutionary job in the world is to be a teacher (of both your own children and of someone else's). I believe that good work—work that you can build upon, stand on, and stand behind—is both necessary and hard to do. I believe in the good and that some of the good that informs my life can only be found in the people who love and support me. I appreciate them—my circle of influence—and I thank them for helping me to see beyond myself. I think in particular of my colleagues at Loyola University Maryland, some of whom must be mentioned by name: Brian Norman, Suzanne Keilson, Arthur Sutherland, Erin Richardson, and Lovell Smith. I am especially grateful to my colleague and friend Martha Wharton, who is good and kind, speaks truth to power, and adds light to darkness. For the past three years, my assistant Megan Fisher has helped with my research and her commitment to my work has been a blessing. I received support, love, and encouragement (via social media) from my fellow alumni from Lincoln University, PA; the University of Notre Dame, Indiana; William McKinley High School (Washington, DC); and from my sorority sisters of Delta Sigma Theta Sorority, Inc. Special thanks must be offered to my dear friends Lajuana and O'Neal Johnson, Debra Newman Ham, and Cheryl Clarke. I am grateful to my parents, Carson and Bonnie Nix Wise, and my siblings, both by blood: Robyn, Labonnie, and Carson, and by marriage: Barbara, Verneal, Eric, Shanell, and Terrell. The road to finishing a book is long and winding, full of potholes and pit stops, broken promises and missed deadlines, friendships put on hold and family outings built around a writing schedule. It is not a job for the faint of heart, as writing is hard, and actively working everyday to share your writing in every possible arena is even harder. With every book that I do and every project that I finish, I am reminded all over again of why I love my children. They are my biggest cheerleaders and the reasons why I do the work that I do—Mercedes Alexandria, Kofi Elijah, and Amir Elisha. My husband, Johnnie, never ceases to amaze me, he is all that I could have ever asked for and the wind that I need to continue to soar. I am, in so many ways, blessed beyond measure and my hope is that I will use what God has blessed me with to make my little piece of forever better.

–*KWW*

\*\*\*\*\*\*

We would like to thank all of the contributors who expanded on the work that was begun in Whitehead's *Notes from a Colored Girl: The Civil War Pocket Diaries of Emilie Frances Davis.* Thank you for accepting the challenge and for joining us in the necessary work of "collecting the ideas and actions of 'thrown away' Black women."[3] You have convinced us that Emilie does indeed have a life of her own and has moved beyond Whitehead's book to take her place within the canon of significant and important nineteenth-century black women. You have shown us that the work to illuminate and explore the life and experiences of Emilie has just begun and future scholars (what Whitehead labels as "forensic herstorical investigators") will be building on the work that was begun by Whitehead and expanded upon by you and other scholars.[4] We also thank Dean La Vonne I. Neal, who continues to mentor and encourage us to think and dream big. She has set the bar for success high and our goal is continue to create work that gets us closer to reaching it. Special thanks to Calvin Coleman for the amazing cover (he is what pure talent looks like when it has a paintbrush and a canvas!) and, to our publisher Kevin Atticks, who is both patient and kind. We are grateful to every family member, friend, and colleague who listened to us ramble on about the project and who made suggestions and offered ideas. Finally, we are also grateful to every teacher who works at the margins, silently pushing the boundaries of knowledge. We see you—with the same spirit of compassion and empathy that wearied warriors have when they meet one another on the battlefield. We developed this text for you and for your students; our hope is that you will find a lesson or two that will transform your classroom into a place of energy, enlightenment, curiosity, and adventure.

*–KWW/CDG*

# Rethinking Emilie: An Introduction

## Conra D. Gist and Karsonya Wise Whitehead

With the increasingly high stakes nature of teaching in schools there appears to be very little room for incorporating books other than texts that are already embedded in the school curriculum. Despite this challenge, as scholars we are committed to developing research agendas and writing and teaching resources that advance liberatory educational possibilities for non-dominant and marginalized communities. We do not have the option to resign in the face of difficulty or the luxury to hold our work hostage as we spend years pondering possible directions and solutions—because, we create scholarship not simply for ourselves but for the unseen faces of people who depend on the unwavering commitment of scholars who take up justice work. We know that the ongoing work to rescue and reclaim the history and lives of black women is important and that it is our duty—in the same vein as Alice Walker's early work to rescue Zora Neale Hurston—to collect and share their life and experiences "for the future of our children…if necessary, bone by bone."[5] This critical restoration work completed in the archives and then shared at the dinner tables, in book clubs, and more importantly, in classrooms seeks to advance Paulo Freire's idea of "conscientization," opening it up and then expanding upon it.[6]

At the same time, we understand (and respect) that there is a necessary gulf that exits between the researcher and the teacher to ensure that every "good" research idea is not then tested on children, particularly those who exist precariously on the edge where the challenge of getting a good education is a daily struggle. So with these multiple streams of knowing in mind, we wrestled with how a critical knowledge project like *Notes from a Colored Girl: The Civil War Pocket Diaries of Emilie Frances Davis* could get into the hands of teachers, and subsequently into the hands and hearts of their students. Simply articulating the virtues of the book would not be enough to attract a substantial readership particularly

1

in our current electronic environment where there are a cacophony of voices and resources vying for our attention. Instead, we reasoned that pairing *Notes* with lesson plans could equip teachers with a vision and tools for introducing and investigating the text in the classroom. This could eventually lead to students having the book in hand and a noble readership could begin to grow. Thus, the *Rethinking Emilie Frances Davis: Lesson Plans for Teaching Her 1863-1865 Pocket Diaries* writing project was launched with this plan in mind.

Since we aimed to develop a companion reader that focused on various ways to use *Notes* across a range of content areas and grade levels, the book was the conceptual starting point for all the curriculum designers who contributed lesson plans. Due to the variety of content area foci, and big ideas grounding the lesson plans, each set takes students on different learning paths but collectively the lessons represent multidimensional instructional opportunities for teaching *Notes*. The tie that binds them together is that they each use the life of Emilie Frances Davis, as discussed in *Notes* and in other sources, as a starting point to construct learning experiences for students. As a whole the lessons demonstrate that rigorous and scholarly knowledge produced about and by black women matters. The "absence" of Black women from mainstream high school U.S. history texts is not only disturbing, but also problematic in the twenty-first century classroom.[7] The erasure and omission of diverse views and perspectives in academic texts is a distortion that communicates an unspoken message to students that only certain groups of people matter in history. Organizing the development of lesson plan ideas for teaching *Notes* challenges this deceptive practice and supplements the critical knowledge project launched by Whitehead, and we hope, empowers teachers to identify diverse and fruitful entry points to learning.

We recognize that the research into the life of Emilie Frances Davis—unlike the multiple streams of research that currently exists about the lives of such black women as Harriet Tubman, Charlotte Forten, Ida Bell Wells Barnett, or Maria Stewart, to name just a few—is just beginning. It is organic and will continue to shift and grow and be corrected and disputed as new information is added and new conclusions are made.

This is the work that comes with being a forensic herstorical investigator, the ongoing feelings of concern that your story has no end and only a comma can be placed where you desperately want a period to rest. Instead of waiting until everything about the life of Emilie Frances Davis has been written, we decided to invite teachers and students into the beginning of this conversation, fully aware that by having them participate in and add to this growing body of knowledge, they are starting the work of becoming active agents in their own knowledge process.[8] We submit that Emilie Davis's life can be viewed through a transdisciplinary lens and that teachers can work both across disciplines and beyond their own discipline to help students connect the life of a freeborn nineteenth-century black woman to their own.

With this in mind, throughout this book, *transdisciplinarity* is applied in three ways: 1) as a quilted narrative (and like quilts, these lesson plans are comprised of various patches from Emilie's life and experiences to create a whole) that provides an opportunity for different disciplinary perspectives to be integrated to depict a meta-narrative of knowledge and teaching; 2) as a guide on the road to freedom (and like the multiple and divergent paths humans pursue to live free and self-actualized lives, the road is ever changing) this companion reader offers different paths for pursuing knowledge and teaching; and, 3) as a tool for pedagogical practice (and like core keys they transcend and open up various disciplinary perspectives) these works emphasize critical thinking and habits of mind vital to all teaching and learning endeavors.

### Quilted Narratives

The lesson plan sets in this reader are organized in two sections. The first, Quilted Stories, begins with Whitehead's article *Forensic Herstorical Investigation: Redefining Emilie*, an ongoing story, and contains five lesson plan sets in the areas of social studies, history, literacy, and English Language Arts that knit together ideas on forensic herstorical investigation, nineteenth-century writing practices, literacy for freedom, and free black communities during the Civil War. In her article, Whitehead defines and explains what it means to be a forensic herstorical investigator as she takes the reader through her process of active engagement and close reading of the text. Using her article, *They Both Got History: Using Diary Entries to Analyze the Written Language and Historical Significance of Free Black Philadelphia* (the first article ever written about the diaries of Emilie Davis), Whitehead illustrates how Emilie's story grew as new information was found.[9] She discusses some of the challenges that she encountered as she slowly worked to transcribe Emilie's diary from her black and white copies and use forensic tools to do archival excavation to find Emilie in the annals of nineteenth-century history. Forensic herstorical investigation, as Whitehead defines it, is a new practice that she developed where the fields of "social history, journalism, diary writing, women's studies, and documents editing meet and coalesce." In the accompanying lesson plan, *They All Got History: Notes on Becoming a Forensic Herstorical Investigator*, Whitehead uses the diaries of Emile, Charlotte Forten, Ida Bell Wells-Barnett, and Alice Dunbar Nelson to teach students how to apply the tools of forensic herstorical investigation to examine nineteenth-century writing practices.

In *Exploring Beliefs and Values in Primary Sources during the Civil War*, Paula Stanton offers a lesson that explores the roles and experiences of people, especially women, in the North and South during the Civil War. Using the work of Emilie Davis, along with the Emancipation Proclamation, Annie Burton's *Memories of Childhood's Slavery Days*, and quotes from Frederick Douglass, students will compare and contrast these sources to determine the effectiveness of this critical document. In a similar fashion, Jeanine Williams in *"Up From Slavery": Literacy at the Pathway to Freedom* has students using various primary sources, including Emilie Davis, Frederick Douglass, Malcolm X, and Barak Obama—to both explore and scrutinize literacy in the lives of African Americans during the time when the Emancipation Proclamation was released; when the Civil Rights Movement happened; and, during the inauguration of the first black President. The final lesson plan in this first section utilizes an active learning approach where students are introduced to primary sources to help them to understand how historians use them to get a more complete view of the past. In *As She Sits Down to Write...: Using Primary Sources* to *Understand the Part*, Noël Voltz has students actively engaging with entries from Emilie Davis's diary, interpreting and deconstructing them, and then having them creating their own pocket diary.

**On the Road to Freedom**

Building upon the work outlined in the first section, the lesson plans in The Road to Freedom use the Emilie Davis diaries to explore a multitude of ways that Emilie and the free black community pursued and claimed political, social, and economic freedom. Covering the content areas of math, literacy, social studies, and history, Section II is designed to both engage and challenge students to think and look for history beyond the "circle of normalcy" (that is, those who are white, male, and privileged) to the lives of historically oppressed groups and the freedom journeys they embarked upon. The section begins with Gist's essay, *A Black Feminist Interpretation: Reading Life, Pedagogy, and Emilie*, where she demonstrates how "reading life through the lens of black feminism offers the reader an analytical framework for interpreting the social world." This essay begins with portraying a possible view of life without a black feminist lens, goes on to consider how black feminist thought can inform pedagogical practice, and ends by exploring Whitehead's scholarship on the life of Emilie Davis through a black feminist lens. In the accompanying lesson plan, Gist outlines for the teacher and student how to actively use a black feminist lens to explore, research, interpret, and evaluate both historical and contemporary texts. Gist seeks to have students wrestle with the meaning of black feminism and ultimately, draw conclusions about the significance of black feminism as an area of study. In *A Gateway to Freedom: Using the Diary Entries of Emilie Frances Davis to Explore Life, Liberty and Freedom*, Whitehead uses Emilie's entries from April 14-April 23, 1865 (the week that Abraham Lincoln was assassinated and his coffin and hearse came through Philadelphia) to explore what life was like for a young, single, free black woman. Whitehead outlines the steps needed for students to become forensic herstorical investigators as they learn how to become an active agent in the production of new knowledge. Students will add to Emilie's story while learning how to write their own.

In *The Free Black Community and The Civil War*, Beau Lindesmith and Kelly D. Selby use multiple entries from Emilie Davis's diaries to complicate and disrupt the familiar stories about the Civil War that fail to include people of color. Labonnie J. Wise offers a very different perspective in *FUNctioning a Dress in Style*, the only lesson that provides students with an opportunity to apply their knowledge of unit rates to solve real-life math problems. Since Emilie Davis was a seamstress, Wise uses those particular entries to explore measurement conversions and proportional reasoning.[10]  In the same vein of pushing Emilie's diaries beyond social studies and history, Rebecca D. Hunt and Joseph E. Flynn, Jr. in *The Ordinary Made Extraordinary: Understanding Diary-Writing and Living Through History With Emilie Davis* have students consider how Davis's diary entries were a precursor to the contemporary forms of diary writing found on social media (i.e. blogs, Twitter, Facebook, etc.). By rethinking and repositioning Emilie Davis's diary entries as Tweets and status updates, students begin to explore both the importance of diary writing and appreciating and recording ones day-to-day activities as being a part of a larger, national history. Lastly, Kent A. McConnell in *Exploring the Democratic Narratives of Free Black Women* offers a final look at the life of Emilie Davis using cultural and scientific methodology. Students examine the entries of Davis along with excerpts from W.E.B. Du Bois's *Black Reconstruction in America 1860-1880* to understand how Emilie may have thought about the problem of race and class in America.

**Pedagogical Practices**

The same sources—Emilie Frances Davis and her 1863-1865 pocket diaries—and ten different ways that it can be explored. This is how we define transdisciplinarity, being able to take one single source and having the ability to effectively use it across and beyond multiple disciplines.[11] Taken separately, teachers have lesson plans, discussion questions, essays, primary sources, and media links that can be used throughout the year to actively insert the life and voice of a free black woman into every discussion. Taken together, teachers have a teaching and resource guide that can be taught systematically (or thematically) offering students multiple opportunities to engage in and use skill sets from all of the content areas. In a broader sense, given the content focus in *Notes*, we envision the lesson plan sets being applied in the spirit of culturally responsive pedagogy, which Geneva Gay describes as validating, multidimensional, empowering, transformative, and emancipatory.[12] Our commitment to the social justice project of education compels us to challenge teachers to closely read the lesson plan sets with an eye attentive to places where transformative and emancipatory learning possibilities are ripe. The lesson plan sets in the reader are initial ideas but not representative of the totality of instructional options for using *Notes* to design culturally responsive learning experiences. In fact, it will be important for teachers to integrate the lesson content in ways that honor diverse knowledge(s), assessment systems and learners in their classroom, which means that adaptations will be necessary.

Additionally, we encourage teachers to join us in the critical knowledge process by creating their own lesson plans based upon the Emilie Davis diaries and adding them to this active stream of consciousness. We envision multiple ways of using Emilie's diaries to teach lessons where content areas converge and overlap; as with visual and performing arts (How can Emilie's life story be set to music? How can we create an oral documentary or a webisode about her life?); or physical education, math, and environmental science (Since Emilie walked everywhere, how can we use maps to predict how far she walked in a given week and to determine how healthy she may have been as a result of this? How can we then take this information to study the environment to determine how pollution— or the lack of it—may have affected her as well?); in technology and science (How can we create an electronic diary where students can become gazetteers to compare their current weather patterns with Emilie's?); or in forensic herstorical investigation and genealogy (How can we use the growing body of knowledge and information about Emilie Frances Davis to deconstruct her life and connect her more closely to our time?). The same sources—Emilie Frances Davis and her 1863-1865 pocket diaries—and multiple entry points for discussion and engagement.

Finally, we cannot ignore the fact that teachers are often concerned about adhering to school curriculum mandates and have little time to develop resources that adhere to professional standards. To address this concern, we organized the lesson plans in a user-friendly fashion that outlines the overview and scope and sequence at the beginning of the lesson. Each lesson plan set also integrates standards, learning objectives, essential questions, and sequencing and time suggestions that frame the organization of activities and assignments in a coherent fashion. Various modes of assessment are offered across the lesson plan collection and two articles are included to offer a foundational text for each of the sections. Numerous instructional design approaches abound in the educational enterprise of curriculum development, and we acknowledge that others may argue for a more or less prescriptive planning template or unit of study model than what we offer in our collection. However, we believe the lesson plan sets included in *Rethinking Emilie Frances Davis* provide a teaching and learning arc that can be easily incorporated in time strapped classrooms with competing curricular demands. We did not make these decisions lightly, every step along the way was intentional and thought out. We wanted to offer teachers lesson plan sets that attended to mean making and transfer learning goals that work to facilitate deep student understanding. We wanted to build on Whitehead's work, fully aware that though her book, *Notes from a Colored Girl*, is finished; the work on Emilie Frances Davis, as an active agent in her own life and story, has just begun. Our short instructional cycle of lesson plans represent the first effort that allows students to use *Notes* and Davis's entries to deeply explore big ideas and evaluate their understanding in a final assessment task in an abbreviated time frame. The same sources—Emilie Frances Davis and her 1863-1865 pocket diaries—and multiple opportunities to engage with it and think beyond it.

# Letters, Lyrics, and Poems: A 'Songversation' about Emilie Frances Davis's Diaries

**Alicia L. Moore and La Vonne I. Neal**

Historically, a diary has been an instrument of solace, a non-judgmental friend, and a consistent companion that listens to one's whispers, words, and tears. A diary is a friend that celebrates the beauty of its writer's life; while simultaneously calming the trials of her life. *Rethinking Emilie Frances Davis: Lesson Plans for Teaching Her 1863-1865 Civil War Pocket Diaries* by Karsonya Wise Whitehead and Conra D. Gist is an ideal companion text to Whitehead's book, *Notes from a Colored Girl The Civil War Pocket Diaries of Emilie Frances Davis.* It serves as a guide on how to care for a friend, the friend being Davis's diary. We extend the friend metaphor a bit farther as we reframe her pocket diaries as a set of songs, which capture the lyrical qualities of herstoriography. As a companion to *Notes from a Colored Girl,* this guide documents a contemporary herstoriography through songversations about Davis's lyrical pocket diaries.

Throughout history, songs have been a source of strength and spiritual inspiration that helped herstoriographers understand the lived experiences of African Americans in the antebellum and post-antebellum eras. Generations of African Americans have expressed their faith, struggles, hopes, and dreams through songs and spirituals. Davis's writings are filled with the same lyrical qualities expressed in African American songs as she recounts the events in her life, which intersect with the Civil War, the assassination of Abraham Lincoln, the Emancipation Proclamation, and the abolition of slavery in real time. The friendship theme, interspersed with reflections on political and religious events, is a continuous thread throughout her writing. Her strong community ties and concern for others' health is present in her daily diary entries. To be specific, Davis records the comings and goings of neighbors, family members, and friends in her religious community. She describes with suspense, periods of longing for her friends' letters to arrive. She recounts with joy, the excitement of responding to those letters. As part of the songversation, we share a lyrical excerpt from Davis's diary—in particular—a poem she wrote in 1863 about the importance of friendship:

*Oh, if I had a kind friend*
*A friend that I could trust*
*It would be a source of joy to me*
*To know that I was blest*
*With one in whom I could confide*
*My secrets hopes and fears*
*And who would not in coldness turn*
*From me in furture years*
*But, oh I fear I never shall*
*Have that consoling thought*
*To help me on through lifes cold stream*
*Though very close I've sought*[13]

Davis's yearning for a kind, trustworthy friend in this poem reinforces the importance of having a companion text to Whitehead's *Notes from a Colored Girl*. Her poem speaks to the importance of handling something as intimate as a personal diary with care, which is an integral part of the herstorical songversation. In response to Davis's poem, we think about Grammy Award-winning singer and songwriter India Arie whose song diaries are a contemporary reflection of the global struggle for human rights and social justice. Like Davis, Arie's work is influenced by the personal and herstorical events of her time. Arie's lyrics from her song, "Just Do You" reflect the spirit of Emilie Frances Davis as she continues the songversation:

*I heard a voice that told me I'm essential*
*How all my fears are limiting my potential*
*Said it's time to step into the light and*
*Use every bit of the power I have inside*
*So what'chu waiting on*
*Who You waiting for*

*If You don't take a chance; You'll never know what's in store*
*Just Do You (Somebody's got to be a star)*
*Just Do You (Somebody's got to raise the bar)*
*Just Do You (Somebody's got to change the game)*
*Just Do You (Today)*[14]

In *Notes from a Colored Girl*, Whitehead provides a transcription of Davis's diaries and reconstructs her life by exploring her worldviews and politics, her perceptions of both public and private events, her personal relationships, and her place in Philadelphia's free Black community during the nineteenth-century. Whitehead inspires us to think beyond isolated events and use the songs of a herstorical figure, Emilie Frances Davis, as a heuristic device to understand the complexities and nuances of the Civil War, the Day of Jubilee, Abraham Lincoln's funeral, and the everyday struggles and sacrifices of colored soldiers and their families.

The Whitehead and Gist curriculum guide contains articles, lesson plans, photographs, and primary sources, which will assist readers in digesting Whitehead's *Notes from a Colored Girl*. The two books are meant to complement one another and extend the conversations about Davis beyond book clubs and libraries and into the classrooms and dinner tables. Parents and teachers of students on all levels of the educational continuum will find that the lesson plans and primary sources are designed to be used to either teach an entire unit on African American history or they can be used as stand alone lessons to complement units in social studies, English, history, literacy, and math.

On January 1, 1863—with the release of the Emancipation Proclamation—Davis writes that it was a grand jubilee, as in celebration; as in a time to stop and give thanks; as in a moment to reflect on how far we have come; and, how much farther we have to go. With the release of the Rethinking Emilie Frances Davis companion reader, more than 150 years after Davis penned her first entry, we believe that now is also a time of grand jubilee; as in a time to give thanks that the letters, lyrics, and poems of Emilie Frances Davis have finally been added to our national conversation. It is indeed a time of celebration.

# Teacher's Guide

**Lesson Plan Series**

This reader contains ten Common Core aligned lesson plan sets based on and drawn from material in *Notes from a Colored Girl: The Civil War Pocket Diaries of Emilie Frances Davis*. Each lesson plan set includes 3-5 lessons that culminate in an evaluation activity and cover a range of content areas, including math, social studies, English language arts, and library science.

**Grade Range**

The lesson plans are designed for middle, secondary, and postsecondary students.

**Time Approximations**

All the lesson plans include time approximations to help you visualize the components of individual lessons. Each lesson ranges from 60-90 minutes in length. The approximations are based on the activity descriptions and indicated grade levels. However, you will need to make adjustments and differentiate based on students' learning styles, interests, and academic needs. Most of the lesson sets are designed for class sizes of approximately 30 students, and planning adjustments are necessary if your class is smaller or larger in size. Although some of the lessons rely upon technology, most of the material can be found online and copies can be made for your students.

**Materials**

All the lesson plan sets draw from portions of *Notes from a Colored Girl: The Civil War Pocket Diaries of Emilie Frances Davis* by Karsonya Wise Whitehead; therefore, the reader must be utilized in conjunction with the book in order to ensure that students have ample resources to master the lesson objectives.

**Standards**

The standards listed in the chart below consist of middle and high school Common Core Standards for math, social studies, and literacy as well as the NCTE/IRA Standards for the English Language Arts and National Standards for History.

**Feedback**

As you work through the lesson plans in this companion reader with your students, the authors invite you to join them in this critical knowledge process by writing and sharing your own lesson plans or assessments based upon the Emilie Davis diaries and/or any work that is written or created by your students, including drawings, posters, diary entries, and reflection papers. Work may be shared either on the Emilie Frances Davis Facebook fan page https://www.facebook.com/EmilieFrancesDavis or at www.kayewisewhitehead.com.

# Lesson Plan Sets Across the Content Areas and Grades Levels

| Lesson Plan Set | ELA/ Literacy | Math | History/ Social Studies | Feminism | 6-8 | 9-10 | 11-12 | Post Second-ary |
|---|---|---|---|---|---|---|---|---|
| They All Got History: Notes on Becoming a Forensic Herstorical Investigator | | | X | | X | X | X | X |
| Exploring Beliefs and Values in Primary Sources during the Civil War | X | | | | | X | X | X |
| "Up from Slavery": Literacy as the Path-way to Freedom | X | | | | | X | | |
| 'As she sits down to write…': Using Primary Sources to Understand the Past | | | X | | | X | X | |
| A Black Feminist Interpretation | | | | X | | | X | X |
| A Gateway to Free-dom: Using the Diary Entries of Emilie Frances To Study Philadelphia's Free Black Community | | | X | | X | X | | |
| The Free Black Community and the Civil War | | | X | | X | | | |
| FUNctioning a Dress in Style | | X | | | X | | | |
| The Ordinary Made Extraordinary: Understanding Dia-ry-Writing and Living Through History with Emilie Davis | X | | | | | X | X | X |
| Exploring the Dem-ocratic Narratives of Free Black Women in America's Past | | | X | | | | X | X |

# Section I

# Quilted Stories

*This section contains five lesson plan sets that knit together activities for understanding and applying the practices of forensic herstorical investigation, nineteenth-century writing practices, literacy for freedom, and the free black communities during the Civil War.*

# Forensic Herstorical Investigation: Redefining Emilie, an ongoing story

### Karsonya Wise Whitehead

## Background

In 2005, I received black and white copies of the 1863-1865 diaries of Emilie Frances Davis. They were very difficult to read as Emilie's writing is hard to understand, the ink is smudged on some of the pages, and there are quite a few entries written in pencil that were too faint to read. After reading them and discovering (from her August 23, 1863, entry) that was she was a black woman, I decided that I wanted to transcribe her work and reconstruct her story. I started with only a few pieces of information that I gathered from her diaries and organized them into a simple gazetteer's chart:

| | |
|---|---|
| Name | *Emilie F. Davis: In the front of her diaries, Emilie wrote her name two different ways – Emilie and Emlie. I originally selected Emlie as my preferred spelling since this is the way that she spelled in the front of her 1863 pocket diaries. I decided later to adopt Emilie instead since this is how her diaries are recorded at the Historical Society of Pennsylvania ad I wanted to be consistent for cross-referencing purposes* |
| Birthday | *February 18* |
| Where she lived | *Somewhere within walking distance of her church in Philadelphia* |
| Church and pastor | *First African Presbyterian Reverend Jonathan Gibbs* |
| Brother (and his family) | *Alfred, Mary (wife), Frances (son)* |
| Brother, uncle, or father? (and his family) | *Elijah J., Sarah (wife), Elwood (son)* |
| Sister or best friend? | *Nellie, Cristy (her beau or husband)* |
| Beau | *Vincent* |
| Events | *Lectures, Concerts, Club Meetings* |
| Occupation | *Seamstress, Domestic (working with at least four families)* |
| Literacy | *Attended classes in spelling and language (perhaps French and German?)* |
| Hobbies | *Guitar lessons* |

This is where I started. I had eleven facts about her life and a desire to find her. As Alice Walker once yelled for Zora Neale Hurston, many nights I called on Emilie to assist me.[19] She became real to me—I decided that in addition to reclaiming her life—I wanted to transcribe all of her words so that future scholars could build on the work that I had started. At that time, I did not have a name for what I was doing. I knew that I was calling on the methods of history and documents editing and that I was working across multiple disciplines to piecemeal her story together. Since I did not have a either a guidepost or a starting place, Emilie's story changed everyday as I discovered new information, reconstituting these three years in Emilie's life. It was a slow process and it was extremely difficult because I did not have any information on Emilie except what I was finding because Emilie had not yet been resurrected from a sea of forgotten histories. Not until 2012, with the help of my mentor, was I able to name and define what I was doing. I was a forensic herstorical investigator.[20] I was conducting an ongoing forensic herstorical (history told from the perspective of women) investigatory process. That is, I actively used forensics, or tools, to uncover Emilie's identity and activity, which had been buried or lost over time. These tools included dictionaries of common usage, census records, neighborhood directories and other holdings from state archives, churches, and private clubs, and more, which allowed me to do a historical documentary excavation of her life for the three-year period covered in her diaries. Finally, I reconstructed Emilie's "story" from a black feminist perspective (a perspective informed by a person's race, gender, and often, class) where I emphasized and centered her voices and her experiences, more commonly known as historiography. I believe that forensic investigation is the practice whereby social history, journalism, diary writing, women's studies, and documents editing meet and coalesce. It is, at its root and center, transdisciplinary work, in that it is both holistic (in that it crosses many disciplines giving us a fuller picture of what we learn from the information that we have) and organic (in that as we investigate further the complexity of the story continues to develop).

To further illustrate my work as a forensic herstorical investigator, I decided to reprint my 2009 article and make comments within the article to show the places where the story changed as more information about her life was discovered. Additionally, I have added primary sources at the end that I discovered while I was editing *Notes from a Colored Girl: The Civil War Pocket Diaries of Emilie Frances Davis.*

###

# They Both Got History: Using Diary Entries to Analyze the Written Language and Historical Significance of Free Black Philadelphia

In 1972, Labov published a pioneering study outlining how to teach Standard English to inner-city African American students, which openly challenged Basil Berstein's earlier "deficit hypothesis" theory. Labov argued that Black children struggled academically not because they spoke a different home dialect or because they were culturally deficient but because they were choosing to "reject" school as an institution. Although Labov was not the first researcher to study African American English (AAE) [see Krapp (1924) and Kurath (1929) for early work in the field], his research in the field, from as early as his 1968 New York City study, galvanized the sociolinguistics field and sparked an interest in the study of AAE. Since then, the field and the interests of AAE researchers have diverged from purely studying the academic implications of AAE (Fasold, 1972; Labov, 1972; Wolfram, 1969) to researching how and when AAE first emerged (see Montgomery, Fuller, & DeMarse, 1993; Poplack, 2000; Kautzsch, 2002). There are four possible hypotheses about the evolution of AAE as set forth by Wolfram and Schilling-Estes (2006): (1) the Anglicist Hypothesis (1940s-1950s), which argues that "They Both Got History" AAE emerged as enslaved Africans worked quickly to learn the language of the owners—the so-called "language of survival" theory; (2) the Creolist Hypothesis (mid-1960s-70s), which argues that AAE actually began pre-slavery as a Creole and then later evolved when Africans and Europeans began to trade with one another; (3) the Neo-Anglicist Hypothesis (1990s-2001), which extends the Anglicist theory and argues that AAE has now emerged as a separate and distinct dialect; and (4) the Substrate Hypothesis (2006), which argues that AAE evolved as a result of the three other hypotheses but it is currently a distinct dialect and it has always been a separate and distinct dialect.

At the same time, there is an accepted notion that AAE, however it developed, has been growing and shifting since the early seventeenth century (Kautzsch, 2002). The four "phases" of regional growth and development began in the seventeenth century, when enslaved and indentured Africans settled with whites in Virginia; continued in the eighteenth century, when AAE second-language varieties began to emerge and spread; in the early nineteenth century (up until 1865), when AAE, as a "stable" vernacular began to spread; and further continued into the late nineteenth-century post-Reconstruction, when slavery ended and close to three million formerly enslaved and linguistically isolated people migrated from the South to the North into segregated and low income communities. The migratory patterns, coupled with the increased linguistic isolation that had begun and were sustained on the plantations in the South and continued in the ghettoized communities of the North, had resulted in the development of a number of different AAE varieties. One city in particular that had seen the growth of a different variety of AAE was Philadelphia, which also had one of the largest free Black communities during the nineteenth century. In 1986, Labov and Harris noted that the language of the Black community in Philadelphia was markedly different from the language of the white community and appeared to be increasing. In the early nineteenth century, Black Philadelphians boasted the largest per capita income of any northern city outside of New York and had the highest concentration of educated and cosmopolitan free Blacks (Hershberg, 1981). At the same time, these elite free Black communities were not linguistically isolated as they lived in the racially diverse neighborhoods of the Fifth and Seventh Wards; traveled abroad; and came into frequent contact with whites, immigrants of Germany and Poland, and newly freed Blacks in business, social, and political settings (Hershberg, 1981). This frequent linguistic contact naturally shaped how Black people spoke and wrote. The language of these types of communities, these "free Black spaces" has not been studied in depth (see Chisholm, 2005 for further discussion of the delineation of city spaces). At the same time, there has been substantial research and study of the language development of enslaved communities.

Beginning in 1936, the Federal Writers' Project of the Works Progress Administration (WPA) hired student researchers, including noted black anthropologist Zora Neale Hurston and historian Dorothy Sterling, and sent them into the 17 states that had the largest enslaved populations, including Georgia, Florida, South Carolina, and Virginia, to interview formerly enslaved men and women, in an effort to capture the memories and experiences of slavery from those who had first-hand knowledge about it. The study yielded over 2,000 interviews that were partially catalogued and housed at the Library of Congress. It was not until 1977, however, that they were rediscovered and published as primary source materials (Perdue, Barden, & Phillips, 1992; Rawick, 1977). Yet, Blassingame (1975), as well as many other historians and sociolinguists, has contended that the WPA interviews cannot be properly substantiated for a number of reasons: (1) the interviews were conducted by mostly white researchers who were asking black people to vividly recollect sensitive and emotional events that had happened to them over 65 years ago; (2) some of the white interviewers were closely identified or related to the *ancien régime*, meaning that some of the interviewers were direct descendants of slave-holding families; (3) the formerly enslaved, who still relied on whites to help them receive their pensions, were understandably cautious in truthfully and authentically answering interview questions about their enslaved experiences; (4) the questions were written in such a way that it was hard to distinguish between past and present day race relations; (5) the interviewers had not been properly trained in the methods of interviewing; (6) interviewers referred to the formerly enslaved in terms that were reminiscent of slavery, such as darkeys, niggers, aunteys, mammies, and uncles; (7) the formerly enslaved rarely mentioned anti-white sentiments, contrary to the ethos captured in other forms of enslaved expressions, such as in the surviving music and stories; and (8) the interviews were edited or revised by staff members before they were typed and catalogued.

Additionally, some of the interviews have been problematized in both the fields of history and sociolinguistics because the transcribers were told to focus on telling the truth "in idiom" and not necessarily to use accurate pronunciation or phrasing, which likely compromised the reliability and validity of the responses as historical sources (Kautzsch, 2002). At the same time, Kautzsch (2002) found that by combining selected interviews, in which the least amount of editing happened, with Hyatt's hoodoo interviews sociolinguistics could gain an understanding of how and when AAE developed. In the late 1930s, early 1940s, and late 1970s, an American Episcopal priest, Harry Middleton Hyatt, conducted over 1,600 interviews with Black people in 13 states along the East Coast. This material resulted in a number of studies about the use of black magic and hoodoo. Although the interviews were not recorded for sociolinguistic research, they are a valid source because one person recorded them over a period of time and worked hard to create a natural interview situation. As a result, Kautzsch (2002) argues, they are a rich and robust source in the study of Historical AAE.

At the same time, this reveals a huge gap in the field. There is a substantial amount of research about the language patterns of enslaved communities but there is not as much detail (or interest?) about the language patterns of free Black communities. One major reason why is because there are no known interviews with members of the free Black communities. The few written sources that exist are works that were primarily created for publication or for public use (e.g., speeches, editorials, and public letters). Written sources are difficult to use for this type of study because many AAE features are spoken rather than written, but they are a solid representation of what was linguistically possible when Blacks and whites came into close contact with one another (Kautzsch, 2002).

I seek to extend the discussion of AAE and the free Black community to include the study of personal diaries written by nineteenth century free Blacks. Although the known diaries do not provide further insight into the study of Historical AAE, they do provide a rare look at how free Blacks used language in the private sphere. Additionally, it demonstrates how linguistic contact may have shaped linguistic identity up until the post-Reconstruction period, when migratory and settlement patterns dramatically reshaped neighborhoods.

## Data and Study

This then is where the diaries of Emilie[21] Davis and Amos Webber, two nineteenth century free Blacks who lived in Philadelphia, prove to be most useful. Although there have been some studies of these geographically specific speech patterns, such as white upper class speech patterns (Kroch, 1995), Philadelphia speech patterns (Labov, 1994), and Tapia's study on the speech patterns of Puerto Rican children (Tapia, 1998), very little has been done in the examination of the language patterns within the nineteenth-century free Black community. This paper seeks to analyze selected entries from Emilie's pocket diaries and Amos' meteorological journals to illustrate how they used language in the private sphere, and to examine how their gender and their social status may have impacted upon their written language. The themes explored have been pulled from Emilie's pocket diaries and reveal some similarities and stark differences in both of their language choices.

From 1863 to 1865, Emilie Davis, a 21-year old mulatto working-class woman who lived in the upper section of Philadelphia's Seventh Ward[22], wrote and recorded her feelings and experiences[23]. Her daily entries were typically short, three to five sentences, and were written in ink or pencil in a leather bound pocket diary, which was smaller than a diary and designed to fit in a pocket. Emilie's pocket diary entries provide insight into the type of community in which she lived, the people she spent time with, and the activities that were important to her as a 21-year old single, literate woman. Although Emilie was a student[24], who attended night classes at the Institute for Colored Youth, she worked as both a domestic, accepting day work and temporary live-in jobs, and as a home sewer[25], making clothes for friends and family. And as a result, she was able to control both her mobility and her finances. Hine (1994) writes that for nineteenth-century Black women, mobility was a critical dimension of their lives. For enslaved women, it aided those who were brave enough to flee their situations; for free women, it gave them more control over their lives. Emilie was mobile, which influenced the way that she interacted and responded to events happening within both the free Black Philadelphia community and Philadelphia as a whole. Emilie wrote every day, at least for the 1,095 days of her writing that have survived into the present, and perhaps even longer than we know. Although her entries are sparse, brief snapshots of her life, she has given us a tool to analyze the background and history of her worldview in the larger context of nineteenth-century Black American life. In the 1860 U.S. Census, Emilie is listed as a domestic, but she writes in her pocket diary about her occasional work as a home sewer.

Her work pattern, as noted in her diary entries, seems to suggest that she worked as a seamstress when she could secure clients and as a servant when she could not. Emilie's father[26] is listed as a waiter, her mother as a seamstress, and her sister Elizabeth[27] as a domestic. At first glance, it seems as if Emilie's family may have been part of the working poor, as waiters were not always guaranteed a steady and secure income. With a closer reading, the fact that Emilie's father was literate and was able to provide education for both Emilie and her three siblings (Elizabeth, Alfred and Nellie[28]) and that her mother was mulatto and possessed a highly valued skill actually suggests that her parents were part of a small number of working-class Black and mulatto families who were able to secure long-term work. Additionally, Emilie's mother was classified as mulatto and her father as Black. Emilie and Elizabeth were classified as mulatto, which probably meant that they had fairer skin. Emilie's two younger brothers, Edmond[29] and Thomas, were also listed as mulatto. These two racial categories were established in 1850 when the U.S. Census established categories to denote the racial status of people of color: mulatto, which included quadroons, octoroons, and persons having a perceptible trace of African blood, and black. Since instructions were not provided to help the census takers determine color classifications, Hershberg and Williams (1981) conclude that census takers probably made a guess based upon a person's skin color and not ancestry. They also note that in some cases the census taker would see only one member of the family and make a color designation for the entire household based upon that person. If their conclusion is correct, that the census taker used one family member to designate color for the entire family, then both of Emilie Davis' parents were probably home on the day of the Census.

Although Emilie is classified as mulatto, in her pocket diary, in the only[30] entry where she racially self-identifies, she refers to herself as colored. While visiting a church in Harrisburg with friends, Emilie writes, "In the evening, we went to prayer meeting. Had a spirited meeting. Our party were the only colerd people, there was about four of us." (Diaries of Emilie Davis, August 23, 1863) Furthermore, Emilie does not mention anyone else's color unless they are white. For example, in that same diary entry, she continues, "Heard a very good sermon, a young white minister that poke reminded me of John."

As are revealed through both the content of Emilie's diary entries about her educational pursuits as well as her actual diary entries themselves, which are written in a relatively standardized English, Emilie was actively involved in expanding her literacy and her fluency. Royster (2000) states that, for nineteenth-century Black women, the active process of becoming literate meant that they were taking the power and authority to know themselves, gaining the skills they needed to read and write, and learning how to act with authority and confidence based on that knowing. In other words, literacy and fluency undergirded a nineteenth-century Black woman's ability to actively construct and maintain her agency. Indeed, Emilie was part of a very small percentage of Black women who were literate and who consciously pursued education beyond elementary and middle school. The Seventh Ward had the highest rates of literacy for black people in the city. In 1856, 45.5% of all Black Philadelphians were illiterate, but by 1870, the proportion was reduced to less than 22%. The illiteracy rate was slightly higher for Black women, with 21% being illiterate versus 15% for Black men (Du Bois, 1996).

In her daily pocket diary, Emilie Davis wrote about her life through a discourse that reflected both her training and her personality. Her decision to record her life attests to her sense of self-worth and her belief that she was living a life that was worthy of being documented and remembered. During a three-year period from 1863 to 1865, a time when the country was preoccupied with an internal war, Emilie wrote more than 30,000 words about her private life. Her commitment to the task suggests that this was not a new practice for her but rather that these were the only pocket diaries of Emilie's that survived. Because of the language that she used, Emilie's diary seems to have been used as a private space rather than as a public one. Bloom (1996) contends that there are some specific characteristics that distinguish a private diary from a public one, notably that private diaries are typically written without extra-textual information. Since they are writing for themselves, diarists such as Emilie Davis do not contextualize either the people that they come in contact with, usually writing just their first name or a pet name, or the places or events that they visit or attend. Diarists also tend to write into the allotted spaces without interpreting the information. They typically do not "judge" the quality of the event or the character of the people in their lives. Daily entries are also usually written in chronological order. Finally, the diarists often fail to distance themselves from the text, lacking both an authorial image, and the depth and dimension of a biography or an autobiography.

### Amos Webber

At 37 years old, Amos Webber, a freeborn mulatto man, once wrote time belonged to no one (Salvatore, 1996). In 1859, Amos had been keeping a daily chronicle for close to ten years. He began his journals in 1849 in response to the public request by James Pollard Espy, the head of the Department of Navy's scientific efforts, for civilians to record information on weather patterns. His entries record his daily experiences as both a waiter and manager and provide insight into both Philadelphia and the free Black working-class community. Amos' journals also connect to part of Emilie Davis's life, since Amos and Elijah J. Davis, Emilie's uncle, were both members of Carthagenian Lodge No. 901 of the Grand United Order of Odd Fellows, a benevolent society for mutual assistance. Amos wrote regularly every Monday through Saturday, his self-designated workdays, about events happening in and around the city. Amos' parents were freeborn mulattos from Attleborough in Bucks County, Pennsylvania. Since the early 1800s, free Blacks who were politically, socially and culturally active had inhabited Attleborough.

The Colored Methodist Society, which later merged with African Methodist Episcopal Church, had been founded in a house located in the middle of the town. It opened it first public school for Black children in 1820. The school, which also served as both, a planning center used by the men and women of the town and as a major stop on the Underground Railroad, provided Amos with a formal education and his earliest introduction to the ongoing struggle to achieve civil rights (Salvatore, 1996). In addition to being a school, the building was also a planning center used by the men and women of the town. By the late 1840s, Amos had migrated to Philadelphia and classified himself as both a waiter and a private butler. Although he was always able to secure employment, it was not until he became one of the managers of Hart, Montgomery and Company, a wallpaper manufacturer, that Amos was able to purchase a home for his family in the First Ward. Unlike the Seventh Ward or the Fifth Ward, which had more racial diversity, the First Ward was 98% white and 2% mulatto. Amos spent a majority of his time with his employers participating in political discussions, meteorological exercises, and private outings with international clients. He recorded all of these daily activities in his journal, written either as comments, reflections, or rhetorical questions. In addition, he would note events that happened in the newspapers, around the neighborhood or in the sky, his daily meteorological observations. From 1854 to 1904, Amos accumulated close to nine volumes of handwritten notes. In contrast to Emilie, Amos wrote from a more distanced space by not writing in the first person and by mentioning events that he was clearly not directly involved in, like frontline activities during the Civil War.

**Emilie and Amos**

One theme that is highly referenced in Emilie's diary is her relationship with her family and friends. She frequently wrote about her brother Alfred, her sister Nellie and her husband[31] Christy, and her father. On average, she discussed her family members three times a week and mentions spending time with her girlfriends at least four times a week. Emilie never mentioned her mother and only once did she mention her sister Elizabeth[32], both of whom are mentioned in the 1860 Census. Amos rarely mentioned his family and, apart from his co-workers, never wrote about having a circle of friends. As a literate skilled worker, Amos probably interacted with many of the elite Black families from the First Ward, such as the Fortens and the Purvises, two well-known elite Black families, who owned homes in the First Ward. He also probably came into contact with neighbors from Attleborough, as they had high migratory rates into Philadelphia. Emilie's journals appear to be much more reflective on the surface; however, Amos deliberately chronicles certain political and social events. He does not record everything but he seems to select political and social information that needs to be recorded. Within Emilie's entries, it almost seems as if there was not a Civil War[33] taking place, a war that was affecting the lives and livelihood of millions of people. Her entries when compared to Amos' seem to project an air of frivolousness[34].

The question then becomes, what did Amos and Emilie leave out? Amos seems to have left out himself, but, according to Salvatore (1996), this was the normal behavior of nineteenth-century men who had middle-class standing and aspirations. As a matter of pride they would never consciously "write" themselves into history. Emilie, on the other hand, seems to have left out the world. Welter (1996) in "The Cult of True Womanhood," writes that nineteenth-century women were slaves to their homes often carving out places where they could express themselves and not be bound by the four cardinal virtues of piety, purity, submissiveness and domesticity. Emilie was probably well aware of these boundaries—young girls were taught early on how to mind their space—and possibly viewed her journals as the only place where she could express herself. On the day that the city is up in arms about the attack at Vicksburg, Emilie gathered all of her girlfriends together and spent the day shopping and sewing. This notion of gathering the women together is fully discussed by Smith-Rosenberg (2004) in "The Female World of Love and Ritual: Relations between Women in Nineteenth-Century America." She writes that in the nineteenth-century female world, the women had highly developed emotional richness and complexity because they bounded together so closely during times of sorrow, grief and loneliness. In addition, Smith-Rosenberg (2004) notes that within these friendships, hostility and criticism were discouraged so that a sisterly milieu could grow and women could then develop a sense of inner security and self-esteem. Perhaps Emilie's choice to be with her girlfriends and then write about it reflects more of what was happening in the world and less about what was happening in her life.

Another factor is Emilie's singlehood. Because Amos was married, perhaps he spoke to his wife about his feelings and reserved the chronicling for the journal. It seems as if he wrote at work because he does not have any Sunday entries. Amos may have reflected in the mornings after reading the paper and noting the weather on the way to work. On the two days that he doesn't journal, a co-worker adds in the information about the weather and signs it (Salvatore, 1996). Since Amos freely allowed someone else to record in his journal, perhaps this is why he did not add any personal reflections or private information about his family. Even though his wife was illiterate, as evidenced by her signing a legal document with an X, she was actively involved in the Black cultural scene. Lizzie Douglass Webber, a light-skinned mulatto, shirt and dressmaker, was born and raised in Smithfield, near Bucks County. Her name was frequently mentioned in the Black newspapers as a frequent guest at many of the city's various cultural activities. She was one of the first women to join the Household of Ruth, an exclusive female auxiliary (Salvatore, 1996). Since Lizzie outlived her husband, there was never a moment when Amos did not have her to talk to or confide in. Emilie, as a single[35] woman, frequently[36] lamented being alone and having no friends. Although she spent a fair amount of time visiting and hosting visitors, she would still constantly write about this feeling of being alone. Her father was very sick and had moved to Harrisburg[37] in early 1863, perhaps to their local hospital for colored veterans, and she wrote about how she missed talking and sharing with him. Since both Nellie and Alfred were married, perhaps Emilie did not see them as much as she would have liked. This then could explain why she confided so heavily "in" her journal. In December 1865, for example, when her brother Alfred died, she lamented for several weeks about her grief and sorrow over losing her brother and her sister-in-law (Alfred's wife Mary died in 1863 shortly after giving birth). On December 22, 1865, she wrote, "Oh Alfred, my poor Alfred is to be buried this afternoon. Oh in my sorrow and in my grief but here I am and all things have passed away."[38]

This openness on the page that Emilie reveals is in stark contrast to Amos Webber's entries. While Emilie often used her pocket diaries as spaces in which to ruminate about her life, her feelings and her relationships, Amos generally focused his entries to issues that happened in the newspapers, around the neighborhood or in the sky (i.e., his daily meteorological observations). He rarely commented about his personal feelings: he only mentioned his wife Lizzie five times, and when his brother died he simply noted, "Sam Webber died this morning about 2 Oclock" (Salvatore, 1996, p. 42) Additionally, when Webber's only son died he wrote, "Harry J. Webber died last night. 10 mins before 12 O'clock midnight inflammation on the brain aged 5 years. 4 mo. 18 day" (Salvatore, 1996, p. 42). Although Webber walked past the cemetery twice a day, to and from work, he never mentioned his son again. According to Salvatore (1996), this private, controlled, and ordered sensibility was normal behavior for nineteenth-century men who had middle class standing and aspirations. In fact, in the few instances that Webber mentioned himself, he referred to himself as either A. Webber or A.W. In another example of his terse writing, on the day his family moved from the predominantly Black and mulatto neighborhood of the Seventh Ward to the prestigious white Fifth Ward community, Webber simply writes, "A.W. moved to Anitast N0 1213" (Salvatore, 1996, pp. 10-11).

In 1863, at the end of her diary, Emilie took time to reflect on all of the major events of the year. She wrote about weddings, funerals, church problems and relationships. But she did not discuss how the Civil War had progressed, what happened with the enlisted colored[39] soldiers or the racial tensions that were happening throughout the city. In 1859, Amos ended his chronicle by noting how the world and the weather had changed. He did not write about how he was doing, what he had experienced or even about how his family had changed since the death of his only son. In 1865, after losing her brother and struggling with the assassination of President Abraham Lincoln, Emilie wrote, "All well that end well" (Diaries of Emilie Davis, Miscellaneous Section, 1865).[40] Emilie's "conclusion," so to speak, suggests that her story begins with idealism in 1863 that, by the end, that story matured into realism.

## Conclusion

Although Amos and Emilie had many similarities—mulatto, free-born, literate, living in Philadelphia and possessing highly valued skill sets—they viewed the world and their place in it from different perspectives. As much as Amos was a chronicler, Emilie was a diarist. I submit that Amos viewed himself as a recorder of history while Emilie saw herself as someone who was actively making history. Since Amos and Emilie were both educated and literate, they wrote using Standard English with very few traces of African American English. Additionally, they both lived in racially diverse neighborhoods and had frequent contact with whites; Amos worked for a white company and white families, and Emilie worked as a domestic for two[41] white families. As such, I argue that their work stands as examples of how linguistic contact may have shaped linguistic identity within the free Black nineteenth-century community.[42]

## Notes

1. In the 1860 U.S. Census and at the Historical Society of Pennsylvania, Emilie Davis' name is spelled Emilie; in the 1863 Report of the Ladies Union Association of Philadelphia, her name is spelled Emily; but, in the front of her 1863 pocket diary where she writes her name in ink and in cursive, she spells it Emilie. Thus far, I have been unable to locate a birth certificate for Emilie to confirm the spelling of her name; therefore, in this paper, I have chosen to use the spelling used in the 1860 Census and preferred by the Historical Society of Pennsylvania, for cross-referencing purposes.

2. For the Emilie Davis and Amos Webber transcriptions[43], original spelling and grammar have been retained.

###

## Going Forward

During the process of rethinking Emilie, I realized that even though I have been working on her diaries for the past nine years, I still do not know everything about her. I am as intrigued about her life today as I was when I first read through my black and white copies. It is amazing to look and see how my knowledge of Emilie has grown over time. When I first read her pocket diaries, no one knew who she was or what her life had been like. I was searching in the darkness, looking for clues and trying to makes sense of her entries. Now, when I search for her online, I can view copies of her diaries, transcriptions of each entry, articles, and biographies about her. My radio interviews and video clips are now part of the record available to other researchers. [44] As a follow-up to my book, I have received a number of questions about what it means to be a Forensic Herstorical Investigator and about how I cope with writing a story that has no end that is constantly being rewritten by other scholars (in real time). It is both exciting and frustrating: exciting because I wanted Emilie to be introduced to the world, to go places where I could not visit, and participate in conversations without me (as she did in her own lifetime); and, frustrating because Emilie's story is not finished and as much as I may want to place a period or write "The End," I cannot. In the same moment, I am proud to have been the first one to bring her writings to life after they languished for years in a cardboard box in someone's attic and then later in the basement of an archive.

When I published my articles, "'They Both Got History': Using Diary Entries to Analyze the Written Language and Historical Significance of Free Black Philadelphia" in 2009 and "Reconstructing the Life of a Colored Woman: The Pocket Diaries of Emilie F. Davis," in 2011, I knew then (based upon the response by the editors and the readers) that Emilie had arrived onto the contemporary scene and that the best that I could do was to continue to research her, to publish what I know, to correct what I thought I knew, and to invite other scholars to join me in my quest as I continue to reclaim her voice and rescue her story. [45]

# Primary Sources

## Emilie's Death Certificate

*Emilie was buried at the family plot at Lebanon Cemetery (it was owned by her father-in-law, Jacob White and it was one of the few black-owned burial grounds and the only one not attached to a church). George was buried there ten years later and at least three of her children (Emilie, George Jr., and Maria) and one of her grandchildren (Florence) were buried there, as well. In my dissertation, "Reconstructing Memories: A Case Study of Emilie Davis, a 19th Century Freeborn Colored Woman," I incorrectly concluded that Emilie's story ended in 1865. I was delighted to find that she married into an elite family and that she had children and grandchildren (unfortunately, I have not been able to find any of her descendants).

# Emilie's Wedding Certificate (3rd name down)

RETURNS TO BE MADE ON THE FIRST OF APRIL, JULY, OCTOBER, AND JANUARY.

Return of Marriages, from the ___ day of Oct. to the 31st day of Dec. 186_, made to the HEALTH OFFICER, in accordance with the State Laws, by Rev. John B. Reese. Denomination M.E. Presbyterian. Residence 1217 Rodman St. Phila.

| DATE OF MARRIAGE | FULL NAME OF MALE | OCCUPATION | RESIDENCE | PLACE OF BIRTH | AGE OF MALE | FULL NAME OF FEMALE | RESIDENCE | PLACE OF BIRTH | AGE OF FEMALE | COLOR |
|---|---|---|---|---|---|---|---|---|---|---|
| Nov. 2nd | Henry Alexander Matthews Steward | Steward | Phila. Pa | Maryland | 33 | Anna Williams | Phila. Pa | West Chester | 28 | |
| Nov. 15th | John Rumbly Martin Caterer | Caterer | Phila. Pa | Phila. Pa | 33 | Maria Louisa Biddle | Phila. Pa | Phila. Pa | 30 | |
| Dec. 15th | George B. White | Barber | Phila. Pa | Phila. Pa | 33 | Emily Frances Davis | Phila. Pa | Somerset Pa | 28 | |
| Dec. 21st | John Andrew Fry | Whites | Reading Pa | Reading Pa | 31 | Josephine Smith | Phila. Pa | Phila. Pa | 25 | |
| Dec. 20th | Josiah Shenk | Farmer | Bucks Co. Pa | Bucks Co Pa | 27 | Eliza Ann Johns | Phila. Pa | Doylestown | 24 | |
| Dec. 27th | Wesley Howard Myers | Coachman | Baltimore Md | Baltimore Md | 26 | Lydia Thompson | Phila. Pa | Germantown | 26 | |

*This is how I discovered that Emilie—instead of spending her life with Vincent or Nellie, two people that she wrote about almost daily—married George Bustill White. Since she never mentioned that they dated (or that she cared for him), I never thought to look for her in connection to him. On this document, her name is spelled "Emily," so either the clerk misspelled it; this is the legal spelling of her name (which is also how it is spelled in the U.S. Census); or Emilie changed the spelling of her name. I chose to keep my original spelling of "Emilie," because this is how she wrote it on the front page of her 1864 and 1865 pocket diaries. Additionally, this is when I found out that Emilie's middle name was Frances.

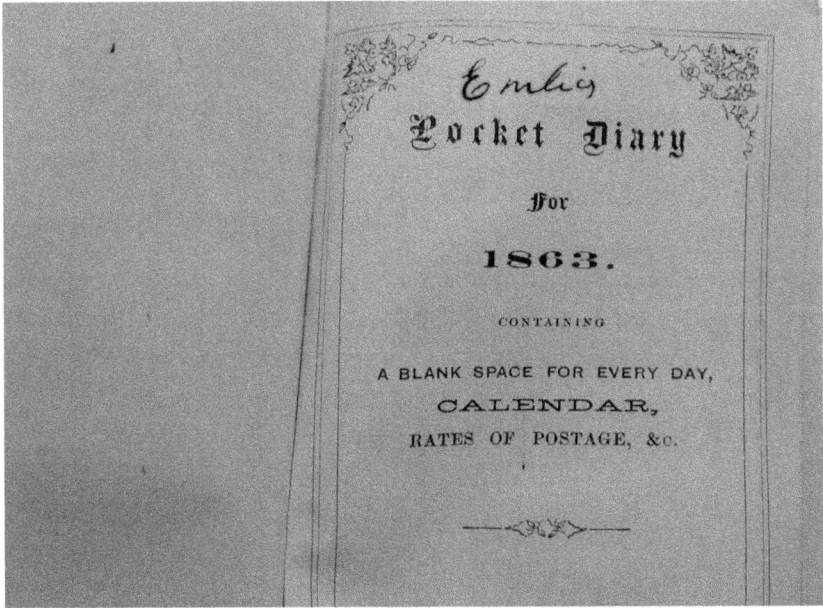

*Here, in 1863, Emilie spelled her name "Emlie" and below, in 1864, she wrote "Emilie F."

# They All Got History:
## Notes on Becoming a Forensic Herstorical Investigator
### Karsonya Wise Whitehead

**Intended Audience:**

9th – 12th grade and postsecondary students

**Overview:**

The history of the free black community in Philadelphia is both complicated and multilayered. Lifestyles, incomes, and church and club memberships were often connected to and determined by a person's skin color. A mulatto person in free black Philadelphia who was both literate and employed wielded a great amount of cultural capital. Emilie Frances Davis as a literate mulatto seamstress was part of a small subset of women who had multiple access to privilege: through her skin color; her ability to read, write, and cipher; and her Grade II skill. During her time, her life was probably more ordinary than extraordinary. She was not a journalist or a poet; she did not speak to diverse audiences or write books; so as far as we know she was an "everyday" woman. At the same time, because her diaries—her conscious act of identity assertion—have survived, Emilie is now considered to be "extraordinary," "special," and "unusual." In *Notes from a Colored Girl,* Whitehead states that even though Davis's diaries speak volumes about her experience living and working as a free black woman, they do not tell the entire story and in an effort to do that other primary sources must be read alongside her work, to collaborate, to correct, and in same cases to contradict. This then is the work of a forensic herstorical investigator, to reach back through time to reclaim lives, to reconstruct narratives, and to fill the gap that exists in our understanding of the lives of free black women. Emilie may not have been extraordinary in 1863 but the process of using her life as a map and her entries as clues, makes this an extraordinary process and in turn, makes her life and her experiences extra-ordinary.

**Scope and Sequence:**

This lesson plan set examines the nineteenth-century free black experience through a close examination of the diaries of Emilie Frances Davis, Ida Bell Wells Barnett, Charlotte Forten, and Alice Dunbar Nelson. Students would benefit from being taught in a smart classroom and from having computer access. This lesson plan set takes three days to complete, if students have at least 75-minute class periods. This would give them an opportunity to study the primary sources, work together to complete the project, and present their findings. Extension activities have been included and can either become homework lessons or in class activities. Students should be familiar with the differences between primary and secondary sources.

**Historical Thinking Standards (National Standards for U.S. History)**

Standard 3: Historical Analysis and Interpretation

- Explain the influence of motives, beliefs, and actions of different individuals and groups on the outcome of historical events
- Consider multiple perspectives
- Differentiate between historical facts and historical interpretations

**Common Core ELA and Literacy Standards in History/Social Studies**

- CCSS.ELA-Literacy.RH.9-10.1: Cite specific textual evidence to support analysis of primary and secondary sources, attending to such features as the date and origin of the information.
- CCSS.ELA-Literacy.RH.9-10.2: Determine the central ideas or information of a primary or secondary source; provide an accurate summary of how key events or ideas develop over the course of the text.
- CCSS.ELA-Literacy.RH.9-10.9: Compare and contrast treatments of the same topic in several primary and secondary sources.
- CCSS.ELA-Literacy.RH.11-12.1: Cite specific textual evidence to support analysis of primary and secondary sources, connecting

42

insights gained from specific details to an understanding of the text as a whole.

- CCSS.ELA-Literacy.RH.11-12.2: Determine the central ideas or information of a primary or secondary source; provide an accurate summary that makes clear the relationships among the key details and ideas.
- CCSS.ELA-Literacy.RH.11-12.3: Evaluate various explanations for actions or events and determine which explanation best accord with textual evidence, acknowledging where the text leaves matters uncertain.
- CCSS.ELA-Literacy.RH.11-12.8: Evaluate an author's premises, claims, and evidence by corroborating or challenging them with other information.
- CCSS.ELA-Literacy.RH.11-12.9: Integrate information from diverse sources, both primary and secondary, into a coherent understanding of an idea or event, noting discrepancies among sources.

## Topic Background/Materials

**Emilie Frances Davis** was a freeborn seamstress, domestic, and a student. She lived in the Seventh Ward and her pocket diaries were written from 1863 to 1865. She later married George Bustill White (his father was one of the wealthiest men in Philadelphia) and had 5-6 children.

**Charlotte Forten** was a freeborn teacher who was raised in the home of her grandfather, James Forten (a sail maker and veteran of the Revolutionary War), educated by private tutors and was one of the first northern teachers to work with free men and women in South Carolina. Her diaries were written over a thirty-eight-year period, 1858 to 1892.

**Alice Dunbar Nelson** was a writer and an abolitionist who had been married to Paul Laurence Dunbar (a nationally recognized black poet). Her diaries were written in 1921 and 1926-31 (even though her diaries cover her life during the twentieth century, she was born in 1862 and grew up during Reconstruction).

**Ida Bell Wells-Barnett** was born enslaved and went on to become a journalist, newspaper editor, and activist. Her diary covers the years 1865-1887.

**Words and Phrases**[46]

**Black Americans vs. African Americans:** In 1831, in *The Liberator* newspaper, Black Americans spent time debating about what to call themselves. The discussion ranged from Afric-Americans to Americans, Colored to Colored Americans and from African descendants to Africans. Since then, there has been a consistent and on-going debate about what is the best (and most appropriate) term to call formerly enslaved people who were bought to America from the continent of Africa. In this lesson plan, in order to narrow the scope of the ongoing discussion, the term Black American is used instead of African American. This document is specifically referring to black people of African descent and not Africans who have willingly migrated to this country, Africans who were born here but whose parents are immigrants or Africans who have dual citizenship. Additionally, as a form of empowerment, in this document, the word Black, when it is applied to this specific group of people, will be capitalized.

*Dred Scott v. Sanford (1857):* Dred Scott was born a slave in Virginia and had lived with his master in the free state of Illinois and Minnesota for four years. He sued for his freedom and argued that he had become a free man because he had lived on free soil. The U.S. Supreme Court, led by Chief Justice Roger Taney, ruled against Scott and declared that since the Constitution never meant to include "Negroes," they could never be citizens and as such they had "no rights that a white man was required to respect." The decision further weakened the Missouri Compromise and denied Congress the power to prohibit slavery in any federal territory.

*Freeborn vs. Free(d):* The term "freeborn" is used to help students understand the differences between black Americans who have never been enslaved nor were they first-generation "freed" people, and people who were "free" or "freed" and were less than one generation removed from bondage.

Objectives
- Interpret primary sources to identify, understand, and analyze the meaning behind the text.
- Examine the diaries of nineteenth-century men and women to compare and contrast them.

**Discuss and deconstruct the lives and writings of Emilie Davis, Ida Bell Wells Barnett, Charlotte Forten, and Alice Dunbar Nelson. Essential Questions**
- What was daily-lived experience like for free black men and women during the nineteenth-century?
- What is the importance of recording one's own experiences?
- What does it mean to become a forensic herstorical investigator? And why is this important?
- How can diaries be used as an entry point to study and deconstruct history?

# DAY ONE: *Covering the Cover*

**Preparation Work**

Three days before teaching this lesson, tell the students that they are going to spend the next three days reading and responding to a blog that was created. They should 1) read and respond to at least one post per day; 2) research the author and write a one-two paragraph biography; and, 3) create their own blog (either electronically or on paper) where they write once a day. Some of the questions they should consider: What is the purpose of the blog? Who is the author? Does the author have other ways that they engage with their audience (Twitter, Facebook, etc.) and what does the blog provide that is not found on other sites?

The students should be split into four groups and assigned one of the following blogs:

> http://www.blogher.com/user/29/posts (Kim Pearson)
> http://www.huffingtonpost.com/marian-wright-edelman
> (Marian Wright Edelman)
> http://transgriot.blogspot.com (Monica Roberts)
> http://kayewisewhitehead.com/ (Karsonya Wise White-
> head)[47]

**Motivation** (15 minutes)

When students enter the classroom, have them to sit in pre-assigned groups of four (one person from each of the four highlighted blogo-spheres). They should give a one-two minute overview of the blog that they followed and then share one of the blog posts with the group.

Have the students come back together and then have them share the blogs that they created, thinking and answering the following: What types of topics did you choose to write about? If you had an audience, who would they be (other students, professionals, athletes, etc.)? Why is blogging important and how has it replaced (or has it replaced) diaries and journals?

**Procedures** (40 minutes)

Tell the students that for the next three days they are going to "become" forensic herstorical investigators. Explain to them that this phrase, coined by Whitehead in *Notes from a Colored Girl*, is used to describe someone who:

- Uses primary and secondary sources from the past to reconstruct history;
- Centers the voice and experiences of women (e.g. using Emilie's diary to talk about the Civil War rather than using President Lincoln's perspective);
- Uses a *transdisciplinary* approach, in that the research crosses multiple content areas and seeks to find places where the content overlaps (e.g. investigating Emilie's work as a seamstress from a historical perspective to examine both the history of fashion and dressmaking within the free black community and from an economic perspective to predict how much she may have made and spent over the course of her career); and,
- Is comfortable with the ongoing restoration and corrective work that will be completed by other scholars (e.g. understanding and accepting the fact that just because they "complete" project does not mean that the research is completed; they are simply providing a starting place for the next researcher to build on their work).

Tell them that they are going to read and analyze primary source documents in an effort to conduct a historical investigation to examine nineteenth-century writing practices to try and create a narrative about the writer's life. More specifically, they will read primary sources written by four free black women: Ida Bell Wells Barnett, Alice Dunbar Nelson, Charlotte Forten, and Emilie Davis to determine some of the issues that they were facing and how these issues have changed since then (or in other words, are black women still writing about the same issues today that they did during the nineteenth-century).

Using *Notes from a Colored Girl* as a starting point, provide a brief overview of each of the writers and an overview of the free black community.

Refer the students to the Words and Phrases list. Go through the list with them and then take time to answer any clarifying questions that they may have. Tell them that this is an organic list and that while they are working with their groups, they should write note any unfamiliar words and then write them on the list to share during the group discussion.

Explain to them that today they are going to work together to use the cover of Whitehead's book to begin working as forensic herstorical investigators.

Project the cover of Whitehead's book, *Notes from a Colored Girl*, onto the screen and ask the students to study it and think about what the cover tells us about Emilie Davis. Students should take 2-3 minutes to write down their responses and then share out as a group. Since the cover has three images, the discussion includes talking about each of them separately and then discussing why Whitehead chose to layer them:

- A page from Emilie's diary, specifically the week of April 19, 1865. Ask the students why was this an important or significant week. Read the entries from April 19-April 21 so that the students will know that these entries are from the week that President Abraham Lincoln was assassinated. What does this page tell us about Emilie Davis? She attended church, her pastor's name was Rev. Gibbs, Vincent was an important part of her life, and that it was raining, dark, and cloudy during the week. Tell students to turn to page 170 of *Notes from a Colored Girl* and study the photograph of the Lincoln funeral train and then provide students them with a list that outlines the route that Lincoln's train took on its way back to Springfield, Illinois. Tell them to think about what the reaction might have been from people along the way. Tell them that Emilie waited four hours in line, with over 300,000 people to see Lincoln's body – why do you think that she did this? *Extension Activity: students could create a diary written by one of the workers from Lincoln's train that details their experience with bringing the coffin and hearse into Philadelphia.48*

- A page from Godey's Lady Book. Tell the students that during Emilie's time this one of the most popular ladies' magazines. It was published in Philadelphia, had over 150,000 subscribers, and had a $3 yearly subscription book. Why do they think that the author chose to include this page on the cover? Answers may include: Emilie may have written for this magazine or that Emilie may have subscribed to this magazine. Have them study the images from the magazine to determine if this tells them anything about Emilie. Tell them to pay particular attention to the "Sewing Machines" and the picture of the woman sewing. Answers may include: Emilie was a seamstress. (It is not clear whether Emilie subscribed to this magazine but given her interest in and her work as a seamstress it is likely that she probably did.)[49] *Extension Activity: students can map out and create a fashion magazine with articles and photographs.*

- A photograph of a woman that only shows half of her face: Tell them to think about why the author chose to show only half of the photograph. Answers may include: the author wanted to focus on the woman's hands and on her clothes. Tell the students that since the author states that she did not find a photograph Emilie, does the use of this photograph lead people to believe that it is actually a photograph of Emilie? Based upon the author's description that Emilie was a mulatto (fairer-skinned) woman who probably had Caucasian features (a thinner nose, thin hair), could Emilie have looked like this woman? What do the woman's clothes tell us about this time period and perhaps about Emilie's work as a seamstress? *Extension Activity: students could search on the Library of Congress websites for photographs of nineteenth-century black women and select one that they comes closer to fitting Emilie's description.*

- The title: Tell students to think about why the author chose to call the book "Notes from a Colored Girl?" Since the author describes her as mulatto, why not "Notes from a Mulatto Girl?" Either have students turn to page 46 or read them the entry from Sunday, August 23, 1863. Tell them that this is one of only two places where Emilie racially self-identifies. She calls herself *colored*. Ask them to think about what the differences were between being *colored*, *mulatto*, or *black*. Using Whitehead's definitions, tell the students why these classifications were important. Tell them to think about the importance of naming and how many names have been used to describe the African American community. Tell the students that as early as 1831, the African American community has been openly debating about what to call itself and that the names ranged from *Afric-Americans* to *Negroes*. Prior to the Civil Rights Movement, African Americans used the term *negro* and it later became *black*. It was not until the 1990s that the community began to use the term *African-American*. Have them to think about whether naming is important and about why the African American community has gone through so many name changes. *Extension Activity: students can come with an issue that they think is important to the school and create an Opinion Editorial page debating the pros and cons of the issue (issues can include cafeteria lunches, school uniforms, amount of homework, etc.).*

**Wrap-Up** (15 minutes)

Tell students to take out their blog and reflect on which element of the cover impacted them the most and why? *Extension Activity: students can work in teams to design a new cover for Notes from a Colored Girl. These can be posted around the room and students can have a Gallery Walk where they share their work.*[50]

**Homework**

Tell students to read through Emilie's 1863 diary entries, marking any of the passages that they find to be interesting or that they do not understand.

# DAY TWO: As It Is Written, Part I
## (Davis & Wells-Barnett)

**Warm-Up** (10 minutes)

Have students share out their blog reflections from yesterday reminding them of some of the key points that the discussed about Emilie Davis.

**Procedures** (10 minutes)

Tell students that today they are going to begin to read through their primary source package to explore writing practices and life in free black Philadelphia. Have them share out what they think they might learn about what life was like during that time. If necessary, give them a short Lecture Blast highlighting some of the key points. Notes should be written on the front board so that students can refer back to them throughout the lessons.

Next, have students move back into the groups that they worked with yesterday and then give a primary source package to each of the groups (the package should consist of selected writings from each of the women) along with several copies of the Text Analysis Worksheet (every student should get their own sheet).

Tell the students to read through the Text Analysis Worksheet and fill out #1 in each box using the information they gathered yesterday from the cover of *Notes from a Cover Girl*.

After working independently, have one-two students share out their responses and answer any follow-up questions. Take time to work through the activity to ensure that every student is clear about the assignment.

Students should then work together to discuss and complete the Worksheets for Emilie Davis and Ida Bell Wells Barnett, using the primary sources in their package.

**Small Group Work** (40 minutes)

While they are working, circulate amongst the groups to make sure that they are spending time discussing the primary sources and working together to complete the Worksheet.

**Closure** (10 minutes)

At the end of the assignment, students should then share-out their findings and discuss how these writings are different from or similar to the blogs that they have read over the last couple of days. Answers should be written on a poster board so that they can refer back to it at the end of the project.

**Homework**

Students should create a blog with at least two entries either as Emilie Davis or Ida Bell Wells Barnett.

# DAY THREE: As It Is Written, Part II (Forten & Nelson)

**Warm-Up (10 minutes)**

Have students share out and discuss their homework blog reflections.

**Procedures** (15 minutes)

Tell students to take out their notes from yesterday and share out about Emilie and Ida Bell Wells-Barnett. Notes should be written on the front board so that students can make adjustments to their sheets.

Next, have students move back into their working groups to complete the Worksheets for Alice Dunbar Nelson and Charlotte Forten, using the primary sources in their package.

**Small Group Work** (40 minutes)

While they are working, circulate amongst the groups to make sure that they are spending time discussing the primary sources and working together to complete the Worksheet.

**Closure** (10 minutes)

At the end of the assignment, students should then share-out their findings and discuss how these writings are different from or similar to the blogs that they have read over the last couple of days. Answers should be written on a poster board so that they can refer back to it at the end of the project.

**Homework**

Students should create a blog with at least two entries either as Charlotte Forten or Alice Dunbar Nelson.

## DAY FOUR: *Forensic Herstorical Investigation*

**Warm-Up (10 minutes)**

Have students share out and discuss their homework.

**Procedure** (40 minutes)

Tell students that today they are going to discuss and debate some of the issues that were important to free black women in the nineteenth-century and women today (based upon the blog posts).

Split the class into two groups and tell them to make a list of 5-7 topics that they think would be important to the women that they are representing.

Collect all of the topics. Tell the students that during the debate, you will call out a topic and students will have 1-2 minutes to decide how their women would have felt and responded to the issues.

**Wrap-Up** (15 minutes)

Give the students ten minutes to reflect on the activity thinking about what they have learned about the writing practices of nineteenth-century free black women.

# Primary Source Documents

**Emilie F. Davis**

> Oh, if I had a kind friend
> A friend that I could trust
> It would be a source of joy to me
> To know that I was blest
>
> With one in whom I could confide
> My secrets hopes and fears
> And who would not in coldness turn
> From me in furture years
>
> But, oh I fear I never shall
> Have that consoling thought
> To help me on through lifes cold stream
> Though very close I've sought
>
> To find this jewel of a friend
> That poets so applaud
> And as I have not found one yet
> I fear it is all a fraud.

*– January 1863*

*Thursday, January 1, 1863*

To day has bin a memorable day. I thank God I have bin here to see it. The day was religiously observed, all the churches were open. We had quite a Jubilee in the evening. I went to Joness to a party, had a very blessest time.

*Friday, January 2, 1863*

Beautiful day, Nellie was up and spent part of the day. Reading (Redding B. Jones) was here. Nellie had an engagement and had to go home. I stoped home a few minutes. The girls were all there.

*Saturday, January 3, 1863*

Very pleasant this morning, buisy all day. Redding on his wer (way) here to service. I went down home to see if Father (Charles Davis) had come, and was hurrying away when he came. I was delighted to see him

*Sunday, January 4, 1863*

I did not go to church in the morning. Very good discours in the afternoon. Dave (DeClones) was down. We had a full choir bible class at Gertrudes, very interesting.

*Monday, January 5, 1863*

Quite pleasant to day, Nellie was up a little while. Redding went away this morning. Siminy [seminary] school begins tonight, we all went down. Several strangers were there, I was quite mortified to see so few out. We did not do any business.

*Tuesday, January 6, 1863*

Very dull to day, raining in the afternoon. I went down home. Heard some good news, Tomy (Thomas Davis) is here. I went to meeting, very

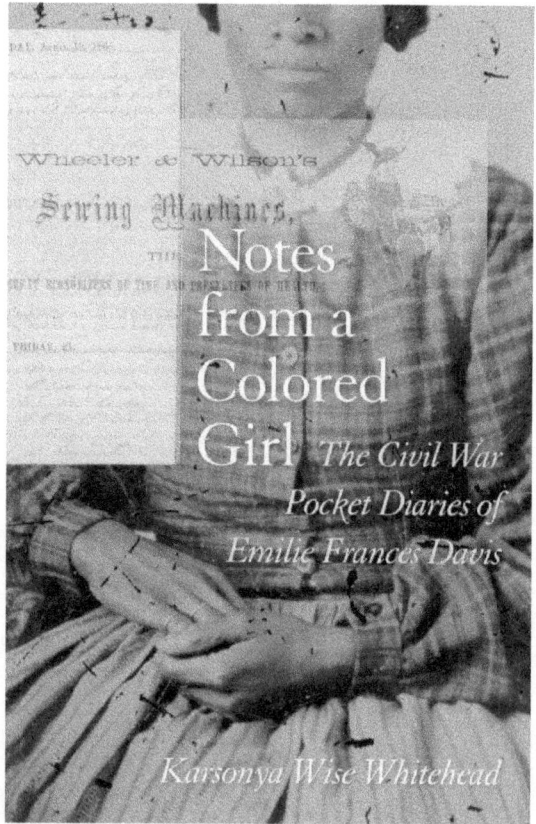

few out, but we had a good meeting.

*Wednesday, January 7, 1863*

The girls called to see me to day. I saw Alfred (Davis) last night, he did not say he sent me the album, but I know he did. Nellie and Sue were up here to night.

*Thursday, January 8, 1863*

Very stormy to day, did not go any were but home and Marys. Liz (Elizabeth Harriet Stevens Bowser) and Stefan at Mrs. Joneses. Nellie bought the long, talked of gloves for Cristy. I spent the evening hour with Father.

*Friday, January 9, 1863*

Very dull. I had a letter from Lile to day. Liz Williams brought it up. Vincent was up here this evening, he bought me a hansome album from a Philadelo (Philadelphia) present. I am deligted with it.

*Saturday, January 10, 1863*

It rained so I did not go out. I was very buisy with my dress. I cut the body out.

## Ida Bell Wells Barnett

The Afro-American is not a bestial race. If this work can contribute in any way toward proving this, and at the same time arouse the conscience of the American people to a demand for justice to every citizen, and punishment by law for the lawless, I shall feel I have done my race a service. Other considerations are of minor importance.

- Ida B, "Southern Horrors: Lynch Law in All Its Phases" (1892)

Booker T. Washington made a great mistake in imagining that black people could gain their rights merely by making themselves factors in industrial life.

- Ida Bell Wells Barnett

Again, the white women of the North came South years ago, thread-
ed the forests, visited the cabins, taught the
schools and associated only with the
Negroes whom they came to teach, and had
no protectors near at hand. They had no
charge or complaint to make of the danger
to themselves after association with this
class of human beings. Not once has the
country been shocked by such recitals from
them as come from the women who are
surrounded by their husbands, brothers,
lovers and friends. If the Negro's nature is
bestial, it certainly should have proved itself
in one of these two instances. The Negro
asks only justice and an impartial consideration of these facts.

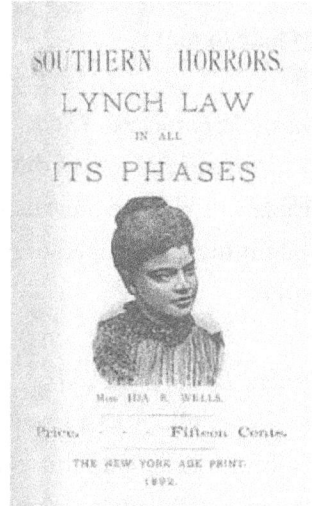

SOUTHERN HORRORS.
LYNCH LAW
IN ALL
ITS PHASES

Miss IDA B. WELLS.

Price. - - Fifteen Cents.

THE NEW YORK AGE PRINT.
1892.

   -Ida Bell Wells Barnett, "Mob Rule in New Orleans"
   http://www.gutenberg.org/files/14976/14976-h/14976-h.htm

Of the many inhuman outrages of this present year, the only case
where the proposed lynching did not occur, was where the men armed
themselves in Jacksonville, Fla., and Paducah, Ky, and prevented it. The
only times an Afro-American who was assaulted got away has been when
he had a gun and used it in self-defense.

The lesson this teaches and which every Afro-American should
ponder well, is that a Winchester rifle should have a place of honor in
every black home, and it should be used for that protection which the law
refuses to give. When the white man who is always the aggressor knows
he runs as great risk of biting the dust every time his Afro-American
victim does, he will have greater respect for Afro-American life. The more
the Afro-American yields and cringes and begs, the more he has to do so,

the more he is insulted, outraged and lynched.

- Ida Bell Wells Barnett, "Southern Horrors: Lynch Law in All Its Phases"
http://www.gutenberg.org/files/14975/14975-h/14975-h.htm

## Alice Dunbar Nelson

No race can rise higher than its women is an aphorism that is so trite that it has ceased to be tiresome from its very monotony. If it might be phrased otherwise to catch the attention of the Negro woman, it would be worth while making the effort. No race can be said to be a growing race, whose birth rate is declining, and whose natural rate of increase is dropping sharply. No race will amount to anything economically, no matter how high the wages it collects nor how many commercial enterprises it supports, whose ownership of homes has not kept proportionate pace with its business holdings. Churches, social agencies, schools and Sunday schools cannot do the work of mothers and heads of families. Their best efforts are as cheering and comforting to the soul of a child in comparison with the welcoming smile of the mother when it comes from school as the machine-like warmth of an incubator is to the chick after the downy comfort of a clucking hen. Incubators are an essential for the mass production of chickens, but the training of human souls needs to begin at home in the old-fashioned family life, augmented later, if necessary, in the expensive schools and settlements of the great cities.

-Alice Dunbar Nelson, "Woman's Most Serious Problem"
http://www.english.illinois.edu/maps/poets/a_f/dunbar-nelson/essays.htm

I have served on boards and committees of schools, institutions, projects. I have seen the chairmen, or those with appointing power, look at me apologetically, and name someone whom they knew and I knew was unfit for a place, where I could have best helped and worked. But they did not dare be accused of partiality on account of color. I have had my offers of help in charity affairs refused, or if accepted grudgingly, credit withheld or services forgotten. I have been turned down by my own race far more often than many a brown-skinned person has been similarly treated by the white race. I have been snubbed and ostracized with subtle cruelties that I am safe to assert have hardly been duplicated by the experiences of dark people in their dealings with Caucasians. I say more cruel, for I have been foolishly optimistic enough to expect sympathy, understanding and help from my own people—and that I receive rarely outside of individuals of my own or allied complexion.

As if there is not enough stupid cruelty among my own, I have had to suffer at the hands of white people because of my likeness to them. On two occasions when I was seeking a position, I was rejected because I was "too white," and not typically racial enough for the particular job. Once when I was employed in a traveling position during the war, I came into headquarters from a particularly exhausting trip through the South. There I had twice been put off Jim Crow cars, because the conductor insisted that I was a white woman, and three times refused food in the dining-car, because the colored waiters, "tipped off" the white stewards. When I reached headquarters I found three of my best so-called brown skinned friends protesting against sending me out to work among my own people because I looked too much like white.

-Alice Dunbar Nelson, "Brass Ankles Speaks" http://www.english. illinois.edu/maps/poets/a_f/dunbar-nelson/essays.htm

## Charlotte Forten Grimké

The long, dark night of the past with all its sorrows and its fears was forgotten; and for the future — the eyes of these freed children see no clouds in it. It is full of sunlight, they think, and they trust in it, perfectly.

-Charlotte Forten

http://www.civilwarwomenblog.com/2007/04/charlotte-forten-grimke.html

*"Monday, October 23, 1854: I will spare no effort to prepare myself well for the responsible duties of a teacher, and to live for the good I can do my oppressed and suffering fellow creatures."*
  -Charlotte Forten, *Diary entry*

*"Sunday, January 18, 1856: But oh, how inexpressibly bitter and agonizing it is to feel oneself an outcast from the rest of mankind, as we are in this country! To me it is dreadful, dreadful. Oh, that I could de much towards bettering our condition. I will do all, all the very little that lies in my power, while life and strength last!"*
  -Charlotte Forten, *Diary entry*

*"Wednesday, November 5, 1862: Had my first regular teaching experience, and to you and you only friend beloved, will I acknowledge that it was not a very pleasant one."*
  -Charlotte Forten, *Diary entry*

*"Thursday, November 13, 1862: Talked to the children a little while to-day about the noble Toussaint [L'Ouverture]. They listened very attentively. It is well that they should know what one of their own color could do for his race. I long to inspire them with courage and ambition (of a noble sort), and high purpose."*
  -Charlotte Forten, *Diary entry*

*"The first day of school was rather trying. Most of my children are very small, and consequently restless. But after some days of positive, though not severe, treatment, order was brought out of chaos. I never before saw children so eager to learn."*
  -Charlotte Forten, *Life on the Sea Islands*

*"The long, dark night of the Past, with all its sorrows and its fears, was forgotten; and for the Future -- the eyes of these freed children see no clouds in it. It is full of sunlight, they think, and they trust in it, perfectly."*
    -Charlotte Forten, *Life on the Sea Islands*

*"I shall dwell again among 'mine own people.' I shall gather my scholars about me, and see smiles of greeting break over their dusky faces. My heart sings a song of thanksgiving, at the thought that even I am permitted to do something for a long-abused race, and aid in promoting a higher, holier, and happier life on the Sea Islands."*
    -Charlotte Forten, *Life on the Sea Islands*

## "Text Analysis" Worksheet

Provide a brief description of the primary source and list two things that you have learned from it.

1. Name of Source _____

What did you learn from the source? _____

_____

_____

2. Name of Source _____

What did you learn from the source? _____

_____

_____

3. Name of Source _____

What did you learn from the source? _____

_____

_____

## "Text Research" Worksheet

What phrases and words caught your attention?

1. _____

2. _____

What was the author's purpose in writing the piece?

1. _____

2. _____

What important historical information does this source provide?

1. _____

2. _____

Do you think this article/letter/entry accurately represents the situation or is it biased?

1. _____

2. _____

What is the author's reason for writing this article/letter/entry?

1. _____

2. _____

If you were able to ask the author one question, what would it be?

1. _____

2. _____

# Exploring Beliefs and Values in Primary Sources during the Civil War

## Paula Stanton

**Intended Audience:**

High School Students

**Overview:**

This lesson explores the roles and experiences of people, especially women, in the North and South during the Civil War as well as the effectiveness of the Emancipation Proclamation. In this lesson, students explore how diaries and other primary sources provided a historical account of the daily lives of women in the midst of such a tumultuous time in American history, and how these accounts and sources reflected the values and beliefs of the writer. Primary sources including the Emilie Davis's diaries, the Emancipation Proclamation, a narrative of the life of Annie Burton, and historical images are examined in order to analyze various accounts of the Civil War told in different mediums.

**Scope and Sequence:**

The lesson begins with a broad conceptualization of the roles and experiences of individuals in the North and South during the Civil War. Students will examine a series of videos, diary entries, a narrative, quotes, and a timeline in order to interpret the beliefs and values reflected in the writing during this time period. After establishing an understanding of characteristics of the time period, students will engage in close reading activities and partner and group discussions in order to examine the beliefs and values reflected in the works. Finally, students will conduct short focused research in preparation for the culminating activity, an on demand argumentative essay, in which students synthesize multiple sources in order to argue the effectiveness of the Emancipation Proclamation.

**Common Core Standards for English Language Arts**

- CCSS.ELA-Literacy.RI.9-10.1. Cite strong and thorough textual evidence to support analysis of what the text says explicitly as well as inferences drawn from the text.
- CCSS.ELA-Literacy.RI.9-10.7. Analyze various accounts of a subject told in different mediums (e.g., a person's life story in both print and multimedia), determining which details are emphasized in each account.
- CCSS.ELA-Literacy.RI.9-10.9. Analyze seminal U.S. documents of historical and literary significance (e.g., Washington's Farewell Address, the Gettysburg Address, Roosevelt's Four Freedoms speech, King's "Letter from Birmingham Jail"), including how they address related themes and concepts.
- CCSS.ELA-Literacy.SL.9-10.1.Come to discussions prepared, having read and researched material under study; explicitly draw on that preparation by referring to evidence from texts and other research on the topic or issue to stimulate a thoughtful, well-reasoned exchange of ideas.
- CCSS.ELA-Literacy.SL.9-10.4. Present information, findings, and supporting evidence clearly, concisely, and logically such that listeners can follow the line of reasoning and the organization, development, substance, and style are appropriate to purpose, audience, and task.
- CCSS.ELA-Literacy.W.9-10.7. Conduct short as well as more sustained research projects to answer a question (including a self-generated question) or solve a problem; narrow or broaden the inquiry when appropriate; synthesize multiple sources on the subject, demonstrating understanding of the subject under investigation.

**Objectives**

- Read, annotate, analyze, and evaluate a diary and a narrative written during the Civil War in order to uncover the beliefs and values of the writer.

- Cite strong and convincing evidence from informational texts in order to compare the values and beliefs in two accounts of Civil War time told in different mediums.
- Analyze the Emancipation Proclamation in order to evaluate its effectiveness.
- Write effective arguments to support claims, synthesizing multiple sources and using relevant and sufficient evidence in order to argue the effectiveness of the Emancipation Proclamation

**Essential Questions**
- How are people compelled to act on their values and beliefs?
- How did the roles and experiences of women in the North and South differ during the Civil War?
- How did the Emancipation Proclamation affect different groups of people based on race and regional affiliations?

## DAY ONE: *The Role of Women*

**Motivation** (20 minutes)

Tell the students that they are going to spend the next three days talking about the roles and experiences of women (and men) during the Civil War. Explain to students that they will also experience how diaries and narratives were used as a means of keeping a written history of historical events, feelings, and actions. Activate prior knowledge by asking students to share what they know about the Civil War and the Emancipation Proclamation.

Next, ask students to create a T chart and jot down what they think the lives of people were like in the North and South during the Civil War. Have students focus on their perceptions of the roles and experiences of women during the Civil War.

Have students turn and talk to a partner about how the lives of these women in both regions might have been different and/or similar to the lives of women both within and outside of military families today.

Show images of women in the Civil War South and women in the Civil War North and have students discuss how these images contradict or support what they already thought about the period.[51]

Tell students that today, they will be reading excerpts from the diary of Emilie Davis, a free black woman who lived in Philadelphia during the Civil War.[52]

**Building Knowledge** (20 minutes)

Explain to students that diaries were key primary sources of information, and served as histories to be read by others. Generally, diaries commented on weather, family life, and sometimes-historical events as they were happening. Model the process of thinking aloud and annotating the values and beliefs of Emilie Davis using the first four days (January 1-4) of her 1863 diary.

Have students read the first month of Emilie Davis' diary entries, beginning with January 1, 1863. As they read the diary, students will annotate the text by writing down inferences that can be drawn about the lifestyles of women in Philadelphia at this time. What did they value? What were their beliefs? How did their actions reflect their beliefs?

## Sharing Evidence from Reading (15 minutes)

Organize students in discussion pairs/groups to share their annotations from the Emilie Davis diaries. Each pair will compare their findings/responses with their partners.

Depending on access to technology, use the white board or document camera to have a couple of students analyze the text in front of the class, thinking aloud and explaining how they drew inferences about the beliefs and values of the Emilie Davis.

## Closure: Writing about It (10 minutes)

Have students use evidence from the reading in today's lesson to respond to the following prompt: Explain how the diary entries of Emilie Davis reflected her values and beliefs, citing evidence from the text in your response.

## Evaluation (10 minutes)

For an exit ticket, have students write down any misconceptions that they clarified in today's lesson on a post-it. Each student will crumple up their post-it and participate in a snowball fight. During the snowball fight, students will throw their crumpled post-its around the room until the teacher signals them to stop. At the signal, each student picks up a post-it and reads it. Have some students share some of the misconceptions on the post-its with the whole group.

Explain to students that tomorrow they will learn about Annie L. Burton, a woman who grew up in the South during the Civil War. Explain to students that as they continue to read different accounts of the same events, they should consider how each woman's political views and values are reflected in their narratives.

**Homework**

For homework, tell students to write diary/journal entries for the next couple of days. In these entries they should write down events, feelings, weather, etc. As they write their journal entries, students should keep in mind that the entries should reflect some of the values, beliefs, and culture of the writer.[53]

## DAY TWO: Comparing the Northern and Southern Experience

**Motivation** (5 minutes)

Tell students that today they will be reading a narrative from Annie L. Burton, who was born a slave in Alabama and later freed during the Civil War. In her narrative, she recounts wartime experiences, and today will be an opportunity to compare the beliefs and values of Annie Burton with those of Emilie Davis. Remind students to take out their annotations from the first month of Emilie Davis's 1863 pocket diary because they will be comparing the two later in the lesson.

**Building Knowledge** (20 minutes)

Have one or two students summarize their learning about the values and beliefs of Emilie Davis from the previous day's lesson before having students read the first 12 pages of *Memories of Childhood's slavery Days* by Annie Burton.[54]

As students read, have them conduct the same type of close reading that was conducted for the Emilie Davis diary entries, annotating inferences they draw about the beliefs, values, lifestyle, and actions of Annie Burton.

**Group Discussion** (15 minutes)

Use a strategy such as grouping sticks (e.g., gather a quantity of popsicle sticks that corresponds with the number of students then randomly group them together to create working groups) to organize students for a small group discussion in which they compare the values and beliefs of Emilie Davis with those of Annie Burton.

Give each group member a role (recorder, reporter, task master). The recorder will write down similarities and differences in the beliefs and values of both women based on their narratives. The reporter will share the group's notes with the entire class, and the taskmaster will remind members of the triad to stay on task and keep up with pacing. As groups are working, circulate to each group to facilitate deeper discussion by asking probing questions and keeping a running record of salient points mentioned by each group.

**Sharing** (15 minutes)

Have each group share at least one similarity/difference between the beliefs and values of Emilie Davis and Annie Burton. Remind students to listen for any ideas that contradict their findings and be prepared to challenge them.

As a whole group, discuss what these diaries reveal about the lives/ roles of women in the North and South.

**Wrap-Up** (10 minutes)

If permissible in your school, use Poll Everywhere to have students use their cell phones to vote on which of the two women seemed to be most affected by Lincoln's signing of the Emancipation Proclamation.[55] This site will show immediate results of the students' votes in a graph or word cloud. If not, place each person's name on a poster board and have students "vote" with their feet (i.e. stand by the name of the woman that they believe was most affected by the Proclamation and then share-out their reasons why).

**Homework**

Have students read and annotate the Emancipation Proclamation for homework and answer the following text-dependent questions[56]:
- What were the limitations of the Emancipation Proclamation?
- Describe the tone of the Emancipation Proclamation. Identify specific word choices that convey the tone and explain how they do so.
- Have students continue to write journal/diary entries. These will be used on day three.

## DAY THREE: Connecting the Emancipation Proclamation to the Narratives

**Model** (10 minutes)

Tell students that today they will make connections between the narratives they have read in class over the last couple of class sessions and the Emancipation Proclamation. First, they are going to share the journal/diary entries that they have been completing for homework with a partner to see if their partner can uncover their beliefs and values.

Begin by conducting a read aloud of the teacher's journal entries as students listen for the values and beliefs of the teacher (or a student volunteer). Ask a few students to speculate about the values and beliefs of the teacher, citing specific evidence from the teacher's journal.

**Partnerships** (10 minutes)

Have students work with a partner, taking turns reading their journal entries aloud as the other partner takes notes on inferences about the beliefs and values of the writer. The notes should include specific details from the diaries/journals that reveal beliefs and values.

**Class Discussion** (15 minutes)

Have a few students share their notes with the whole group. While the notes are being shared, have each pair of students call out one-word values/beliefs reflected in their diaries/journals and develop a running list of them on the board, placing a check beside those that are repeated. Develop a consensus of the beliefs and values of the class as a whole (based on their diary/journals).

**Finding Values Reflected in Quotes** (20 minutes)

Tell students that they will read several quotes from Frederick Douglass, a Maryland born slave, born in 1818. Share a timeline of the life of Frederick Douglass.[57] Post quotes by Frederick Douglass from the video around the room. Have students view the video of Douglass's quotes.[58]

After the video, have students stand beside the quote that resonates with them and/or reflects values that are similar to theirs.

Provide one minute for students at each posted quote to discuss why they chose the quote.

Next, have students move to the poster that least resonates with their values/beliefs.

Allow an additional minute for students to discuss why they chose the poster and how/why they disagree with the quote.

**Class Discussion** (20 minutes)

Ask students to take out the text-dependent questions from the homework assignment and any notes/annotations on the Emancipation Proclamation.

Conduct a whole group discussion on the following topics:

- Describe the tone, values, and beliefs of Abraham Lincoln in the Emancipation Proclamation.
- Discuss how the Emancipation Proclamation affected Emilie Davis, Annie Burton, and Frederick Douglass.
- Have students decide which one of the three people they think were most affected by the Emancipation Proclamation, justifying their responses with evidence from the texts discussed in class.
- Discuss how/whether the Emancipation Proclamation has affected our lives today.

**Wrap-up/Closure** (5 minutes)

Tell students to write a one-sentence opinion statement reflecting on the effectiveness of the Emancipation Proclamation.

**Homework**

Have students conduct short-focused research in which they find articles/information that supports their opinion on whether or not the Emancipation Proclamation was effective.

# DAY FOUR: *Argument Writing*

**On Demand Argument** (60 minutes)

Tell students that they are going to write an on-demand argumentative essay in which they will argue the effectiveness of the Emancipation Proclamation. The essay requires that students do the following:

- Take a position on whether it was an effective document.
- Cite at least two of the texts read in class (Emilie Davis's diary, narrative of Annie Burton, Frederick Douglass's quotes/timeline)
- Use information from a source found in the short focused research homework assignment to support claims.
- Include evidence from today's society to support their claims.

NOTE: Have students write in 20-minute increments, pausing for short 1-2 minute brain breaks between segments. The brain breaks can include a short game of "Rock-Paper-Scissors," a quick game of "Simon Says," and/or a quick dance-off with 30- second bursts of music.

**Wrap-Up** (15 minutes)

Reflect back on the essential questions. Have students work together to make a list of how the men and women of the Civil War Era acted on their beliefs and values.

# "Up From Slavery": Literacy as the Pathway to Freedom

### Jeanine L. Williams

**Intended Audience:**

High School English Language Arts Students

**Overview:**

This lesson explores the role of literacy in the lives of African Americans (Emilie Davis, Frederick Douglass, Malcolm X, and Barack Obama) during various time periods following the end of slavery. The lives of these individuals will be examined as a vehicle for critically thinking about the various pathways to freedom that literacy provides—especially as it relates to self-advocacy and social activism.

**Scope and Sequence:**

This lesson plan series will take place over the course of five days and begins with a broad conceptualization of the role of literacy in society. Using the diaries of Emilie Davis as a springboard, students will examine a series of personal narratives, photos, and videos with which they will make inferences and draw conclusions about how literacy influenced the lives of each individual. Students will scrutinize the role and restrictions on literacy during the Emancipation Proclamation, the Civil Rights Movement, and the inauguration of the first African American president.

**NCTE/IRA Standards for the English Language Arts**

- Students read a wide range of print and non-print texts to build an understanding of texts, of themselves, and of the cultures of the United States and the world; to acquire new information; to respond to the needs and demands of society and the workplace; and for personal fulfillment. Among these texts are fiction and nonfiction, classic and contemporary works.

- Students read a wide range of literature from many periods in many genres to build an understanding of the many dimensions (e.g., philosophical, ethical, aesthetic) of human experience.
- Students apply a wide range of strategies to comprehend, interpret, evaluate, and appreciate texts. They draw on their prior experience, their interactions with other readers and writers, their knowledge of word meaning and of other texts, their word identification strategies, and their understanding of textual features (e.g., sound-letter correspondence, sentence structure, context, graphics).
- Students employ a wide range of strategies as they write and use different writing process elements appropriately to communicate with different audiences for a variety of purposes.
- Students apply knowledge of language structure, language conventions (e.g., spelling and punctuation), media techniques, figurative language, and genre to create, critique, and discuss print and non-print texts.

## Common Core Standards for English Language Arts

- CCSS.ELA-Literacy.RI.9-10.1. Cite strong and thorough textual evidence to support analysis of what the text says explicitly as well as inferences drawn from the text.
- CCSS.ELA-Literacy.RI.9-10.2. Determine a central idea of a text and analyze its development over the course of the text, including how it emerges and is shaped and refined by specific details; provide an objective summary of the text.
- CCSS.ELA-Literacy.RI.9-10.6. Compare the point of view of two or more authors for how they treat the same or similar topics, including which details they include and emphasize in their respective accounts.
- CCSS.ELA-Literacy.RI.9-10.7. Analyze various accounts of a subject told in different mediums (e.g., a person's life story in both print and multimedia), determining which details are em-

phasized in each account.

- CCSS.ELA-Literacy.RI.9-10.8. Delineate and evaluate the argument and specific claims in a text, assessing whether the reasoning is valid and the evidence is relevant and sufficient; identify false statements and fallacious reasoning.
- CCSS.ELA-Literacy.RI.9-10.9. Draw evidence from literary or informational texts to support analysis, reflection, and research.
- CCSS.ELA-Literacy.SL.9-10.1. Initiate and participate effectively in a range of collaborative discussions (one-on-one, in groups, and teacher-led) with diverse partners on grades 9-10 topics, texts, and issues, building on others' ideas and expressing their own clearly and persuasively.

## Objectives

- Examine the role of literacy in our lives and society.
- Analyze and interpret the social and political roles literacy played in the lives of African Americans, namely: Emilie Davis, Frederick Douglass, Malcolm X, Barack Obama
- Synthesize the various ways literacy created pathways of freedom for African Americans.
- Create a critical reflection that makes claims about connections between the literacy experiences of Emilie Davis, Frederick Douglass, Malcolm X, and Barack Obama, and the student.

## Essential Questions

- In what ways does literacy create pathways to freedom?
- What role does literacy play in social and political activism?
- What role does literacy play in your life?

## DAY ONE: *Literacy Pathways for Emilie Davis*

**Warm-Up (15 minutes)**

Explain to the students that they are going to spend the next five days talking about literacy and the role it plays in society—especially as it relates to African Americans during various periods in history. Using a series of visual images of literate behaviors, have students brainstorm and list the characteristics of literacy.[59] Based on these characteristics, determine a definition for the term 'literacy.'

Lead the students in a discussion about the importance of literacy in society. *How does literacy enable us to function in society? What difficulties might a lack of literacy create? As a society, how do we respond to highly literate individuals? How do we respond to individuals who lack literacy?*

Have students complete a 5-minute "quick-write" on how they use literacy in their everyday lives. Then, ask for a few students to share their responses.

**Whole Class Discussion** (10 minutes)

Explain to students that one important aspect of literacy is critical thinking. In a brief mini-lecture, write the following information on the board (or disseminate in a handout) and explain the importance of thinking critically as they read.

*Thinking critically as you read entails understanding not only what the author states directly, but also what the author suggests. In other words, it is your responsibility as a critical reader to make inferences and draw conclusions about what you have read.*

*An inference is a reasonable assumption based on the information you have about an event, a person, or a written passage. Another way to think of making inferences, or inferring, is "reading between the lines." When you "read between the lines," you can often come to a well-founded conclusion, which is probably accurate.*

*A conclusion is a decision that is reached after thoughtful consideration of information the author presents. The information that is given will lead you to the conclusion that should be drawn.*

### Small Groups (20 minutes)

In small groups, have the students read and discuss the following excerpts from *Notes from a Colored Girl: The Civil War Pocket Diaries of Emilie Frances Davis.* Explain to students that during the mid-1800s, in free black Philadelphia, literacy rates were low as only one out of every four households sent their children to school. In the Seventh Ward, where Emilie lived, they had the highest percentage of free blacks that could read and write.[60] In their discussion, the students should consider the role of literacy in Emilie's life as well as the restrictions on literacy—especially for women and the enslaved.

Explain to the students that throughout her diary, Emilie makes mention of her school attendance. Given the role and restrictions on literacy that they discussed, have students make inferences about why literacy was a highlight in Emilie's life. *In what ways was Emilie's life and experiences shaped by literacy?*

### Excerpts from *Notes from a Colored Girl*

*Emilie lived about five minutes from her school, the Institute for Colored Youth (now Cheney University). The school opened in 1837 after Richard Humphreys, a Quaker and a silversmith, bequeathed $10,000 (one-tenth of his estate) to design and establish a school for "the benevolent design of instructing the descendants of the African race in school learning, in the various branches of the mechanic arts and trades, and in agriculture, in order to prepare, fit and qualify them to act as teachers." The institute was known for its rigid entrance examinations, its tuition fee of ten dollars per semester plus the costs of books and stationary, the pyramidal structure of its classes (since passage from one grade level to the next was highly competitive and extremely rigorous, the upper-level classes were much smaller than the lower-level classes)* *and its strong liberal arts curriculum. The school's mission was to train black teachers using other black teachers. Additionally the curriculum included composition, Greek grammar, algebra, plane and spherical trigonometry, geometry, poetry, classics, sciences, and classical Latin. Students had to complete an intensive, difficult examination in geometry, Latin, Greek, and plane and spherical trigonometry.*

*From 1863 to 1865, Emilie took evening classes on Monday night in the institute's seminary program, which included instruction in Bible and spelling. It also appears as if Emilie took language courses in French and German. Courses began in October, and the school had both a winter and spring session. It is not clear whether these courses were strictly for credit or if they were informal classes that were organized to serve the community. Here she mentioned taking language and spelling classes: "I expecte to go home to day. No girls come but I taken French leacn [lessons]"; and "Examination in the afternoon, it was very much crowed. Cristy had a special spelling class in the afternoon for our benefit." She also used some French and German words in her entries. In one example that suggests her knowledge of French, Emilie wrote, "It was a perfect jure" (cf. French jour, meaning "day"). Similarly, in another example, Emilie used a spelling that suggests knowledge of German: "They went down to see the Fralerne" (cf. German fräulein, meaning "young woman").*

*As are revealed through both the content of Emilie's diary entries about her educational pursuits as well as her actual diary entries themselves, which are written in a relatively standardized English, Emilie was actively involved in expanding her literacy. For nineteenth-century black women, the active process of becoming literate meant that they were taking the power and authority to know themselves, they were gaining the skills they needed to read and write, and they were learning how to act with authority and*

*confidence based on that knowledge. Literacy and fluency under-*
*girded a nineteenth-century black woman's ability to actively*
*construct and maintain her agency.*

*In addition to her skin color, Emilie was also privileged because*
*she was literate, which placed here in within a small category*
*of nineteenth-century literate black people and within an even*
*smaller category of nineteenth-century literate black women.*
*During the mid-1800s literacy rates among free black people in*
*Philadelphia were low with only one out of every four free black*
*households sending its children to school.*

*In addition to her leisure activities, church, and work, Emilie was*
*actively involved in abolitionist fundraising activities. In 1863,*
*the Hutchinson Family Singers, the first American close-harmo-*
*ny quartet who traveled throughout the Northeast and England*
*singing and raising money for the abolitionist, temperance, and*
*women's rights movements, was scheduled to host a concert to*
*raise money for the abolitionist cause. Emilie was one of the*
*many church members who sold tickets for this event. On the day*
*the concert was announced, she wrote, "The Hutchinsons give a*
*concert next Thusday night for the benefit of our church." She spent*
*the week trying to sell her tickets: "I have bin very buisy trying*
*to sell ticets for the concert. Alfred brought one." On the day of*
*the concert, she happily noted, "I sold all my tickets. Nellie and*
*Rochel [close friend] over, went to the concert. It was good, every*
*one seemed pleased.".… Although these women had not been born*
*enslaved, they had probably heard discussions about legalized*
*slavery around the dinner table or in their classrooms, and they*
*were probably familiar with the lectures of Frederick Douglass*
*and Maria Stewart, the first black woman to speak to a diverse*
*audience of men and women.*

*With her background knowledge of enslavement and resistance,*

*Emilie's activities on January 1, 1863, provide an insight into
how free black women celebrated the occasion: "Today has bin
a memorable day. I thank God I have bin here to see it. The day
was religiously observed. All the churches were open. We had quite
a Jubilee in the evening. I went to Joness to a party, had a very
blessest time."*

*As a member of the Association, Emilie received firsthand infor-
mation of what was happening in the newly freed black communities. Though she did not record what was discussed, it is not
unreasonable to conclude that they did discuss it and the fact that
she participated in these types of private meetings and abolitionist
endeavors speaks again to the fact that she held social status as
a mulatto woman within Philadelphia's free black community.
Though Emilie did not occupy the ranks of the elite, it is never-
theless clear that she possessed a fair amount of cultural and social
capital, exemplified through her education, her connections to
other powerful members of the black community, and her regular
association with them at social and political events.*[61]

**Wrap-Up** (15 minutes)

Have students write a quick 5-minute reader response answering the
following prompt:

*How did her ability to pursue literacy create pathways to freedom for
Emilie Davis? In what ways did literacy allow Emilie to participate in the
events surrounding the Emancipation Proclamation? (Time permitting: have
students share their responses to the prompt.)*

# DAY TWO: Literacy Pathways for Frederick Douglass

**Warm Up** (15 minutes)

Explain to the students that today they will focus on the literacy pathways for former slave and abolitionist, Frederick Douglass. Provide the students with a brief biographical overview for Frederick Douglass.[62]

Highlighting the following excerpts from *Notes from a Colored Girls*, explain to the students that Frederick Douglass was very influential in Emilie's abolitionist work.

**Excerpts from** *Notes from a Colored Girl*

*Friday, June 19, 1863*

Last night, they had quite a disloyal meeting about Mr. Gibbs. The Trustees were about to turn Mr. Gibbs right out of the church. The meeting was posphoned. It was almost 12'o when we left the church.

*The Trustees included Jacob White Sr., Alexander Guy, Robert Adger Jr., and Jacob Farbeaux. A meeting was held at Sansom Hall to constitute a general committee for raising black regiments. Both Anna Elizabeth Dickinson (antislavery and women's rights' lecturer), and Frederick Douglass spoke and helped to raise over $30,000 to support the troops.*

*Monday, August 10, 1863*

I was over to Chases a little while last night, quite warm. I spent part of the morning with Mary. I wrote to Sarah and Alfred yesterday.

*Frederick Douglass met with President Abraham Lincoln to discuss the unequal pay and poor treatment that black soldiers were receiving.*

*Friday, December 4, 1863*

In the evening, we went hear Fred Duglass. Yesterday, I paid a visit to the White house. I have bin so busy, I did not have time to write.

*The Third Decade Anniversary Celebration of the American Anti-Slavery*

*Society was held at the Philadelphia Concert Hall. The question that served as the theme of the event was "What Would Be the Future of Negroes in the U.S.?" William Lloyd Garrison presided and Lucretia Mott was one of the featured speakers. Frederick Douglass also delivered a speech entitled "Our Work is Not Done."*[63]

## Independent Reading and Discussion (20 minutes)

Have students read Douglass's speech, "Our Work is Not Done."[64] Ask students to react to the speech, and make inferences about Douglass's level of education and literacy.

On the board, make a list of the students' thoughts and reactions. The class will revisit this list later in the lesson.

## Small Group and Discussion (15-20 minutes)

In small groups, have students complete a shared reading of "Learning to Read and Write" by Frederick Douglass.[65] As they read, have students underline and discuss words and phrases from the reading that relate to Douglass's literacy experience.

Based on their reading and discussion of "Our Work is Not Done" and "Learning to Read and Write," have students discuss inferences about the pathway(s) that literacy provided for Frederick Douglass. How did literacy change Douglass? In what ways was his life and experiences shaped by literacy?

## Wrap-Up (10 minutes)

Have students write a reader response to the following prompt:

- *In what ways did literacy create a pathway to freedom for Frederick Douglass? How did literacy allow Frederick Douglass to participate in the events surrounding the abolishment of slavery? How are his experiences similar and different to the literacy experiences of Emilie? In what ways did Douglass influence the life and literacy of Emilie Davis?*

# DAY THREE: Literacy Pathways for Malcolm X

**Warm-Up** (20 minutes)

Explain to the students that today they will focus on the literacy pathways for civil rights activist, Malcolm X. Provide the students with a brief biographical overview for Malcolm X.[66]

Have students watch the video or listen to the audio of Malcolm X's speech "Who Taught You to Hate Yourself?"[67]

Based on the video, ask students to react to the speech, and make inferences about Malcolm X's level of education and literacy. On the board, make a list of the students' thoughts and reactions. The class will revisit this list later in the lesson.

**Small Groups** (30 minutes)

In small groups, have students complete a shared reading of "Learning to Read."[68] As they read, have student underline and discuss words and phrases from the reading that relate to Malcolm X's literacy experience. Once completed, have students share highlights of their reading and discussion with the rest of the class.

Have students review and discuss the following quotes from the text with theses questions in mind: What do these quotes indicate about Malcolm X's level of education and literacy? How might this be different from the students' initial speculations?

> I saw that the best thing I could do was get hold of a dictionary—to study, to learn some words. I was lucky enough to reason also that I should try to improve my penmanship. It was sad. I couldn't even write in a straight line. It was both ideas together that moved me to request a dictionary along with some tablets and pencils from the Norfolk Prison Colony School.

> I suppose it was inevitable that as my word-base broadened, I

*could for the first time pick up a book and read and now begin
to understand what the book was saying. Anyone who has read
a great deal can imagine the new world that opened. Let me tell
you something: from then until I left that prison, in every free
moment I had, if I was not reading in the library, I was reading on my bunk. You couldn't have gotten me out of books with a
wedge. Between Mr. Muhammad's teachings, my correspondence,
my visitors—usually Ella and Reginald—and my reading of
books, months passed without my even thinking about being
imprisoned. In fact, up to then, I never had been so truly free in
my life.*

*I have often reflected upon the new vistas that reading opened to
me. I knew right there in prison that reading had changed forever
the course of my life. As I see it today, the ability to read awoke
inside me some long dormant craving to be mentally alive. I certainly wasn't seeking any degree, the way a college confers a status
symbol upon its students. My homemade education gave me, with
every additional book that I read, a little bit more sensitivity
to the deafness, dumbness, and blindness that was afflicting the
black race in America. Not long ago, an English writer telephoned
me from London, asking questions. One was, "What's your alma
mater?" I told him, "Books." You will never catch me with a free
fifteen minutes in which I'm not studying something I feel might
be able to help the black man.*

Based on their discussion of the video and "Learning to Read," have
students make inferences about the pathway(s) that literacy provided for
Malcolm X. How did literacy change Malcolm X? In what ways was his
life and experiences shaped by literacy?

## Wrap-Up (10 minutes)

Have students write a reader response to the following prompt:

* *In what ways did literacy create a pathway to freedom for Malcolm
  X? How did literacy allow Malcolm X to participate in the events*

*surrounding the Civil Rights Movement? How are his experiences similar to and different from the literacy experiences of Emilie? In what ways might the work of Emilie Davis and Frederick Douglass have contributed to Malcolm X's literacy and activism?*

# DAY FOUR: Literacy Pathways for Barack Obama

**Warm Up** (20 minutes)

Explain to the students that today they will focus on the literacy pathways for President Barack Obama. Provide the students with a brief biographical overview for President Obama.[69]

Have students complete a 10-minute "quick write" where they reflect on the significance of Obama's presidency—especially in light of what they learned about Emilie Davis, Frederick Douglass, and Malcolm X. Ask a few students to share their reflections.

**Video Note-taking** (15 minutes)

Show students a video of Barack Obama speaking about education.[70] Ask the students to make note of President Obama's ideas about the role of literacy/education in his life and in society, as they watch the video.

**Independent Reading** (15 minutes)

Then, have students independently read "Remarks by the President on a World-Class Education."[71] As they read have the students underline words and phrases related to President Obama's literacy experiences and the importance of education.

**Class Discussion** (10 minutes)

Lead the students in a discussion of their notes on the video and the reading selection.

Based on their reading and discussion of the video and "Remarks by the President on a World-Class Education," have students make inferences about the pathway(s) that literacy provided for President Obama. *How did literacy change Obama? In what ways was his life and experiences shaped by literacy?*

**Wrap-Up** (10 minutes)

Have students write a reader response to the following prompt:

- *In what ways did literacy create a pathway to freedom for President Obama? How did literacy allow Obama to be the first African American to hold the United States presidency? How are his experiences similar to and different from the literacy experiences of Emilie? In what ways might the work of Emilie Davis, Frederick Douglass, and Malcolm X have contributed to President Obama's literacy, political success, and his beliefs about education?*

# DAY FIVE: Critical Reflection on Literacy Pathways

**Warm Up** (10 minutes)

Read the following excerpt from *Notes from a Colored Girl* to your students. Lead the students in a discussion of the connections that the author makes between the life of Emilie Davis and her own:

**Excerpts from *Notes from a Colored Girl***

> *In doing so, I slowly began to realize how Emilie's situations, friendships, beauty rituals, and relationship struggles were very similar to my own everyday experiences. I knew that I was working on telling Emilie's story from my position as both an "outsider," from another time and place, who is squinting at her life through a telescopic long view of history, and as a loosely connected "insider." At the same time, since I am from South Carolina and am only five generations removed from slavery, I do believe that as Emilie worked in the North to raise monies for the freedman in Charleston and to help end enslavement, it benefitted my family in the South. I am living the future—with a black president, the legacy of the civil rights movement, and the impact of the Reconstruction Amendments—which she worked for but probably never could have completely imagined.[72]*

**Critical Reflection Paper** (40 minutes)

Tell the students that they will write a critical reflection on the literacy pathways for Emilie Davis, Frederick Douglass, Malcolm X, and Barack Obama. In this reflection paper the students will discuss the following:

- What connections can be made between the literacy and life experiences of Emilie Davis, Frederick Douglass, Malcolm X, and Barack Obama? How did literacy create pathways to freedom for each individual?

- What role does literacy play in social and political activism?
- What personal connections might you make with the literacy and life experiences of Emilie Davis, Frederick Douglass, Malcolm X, and Barack Obama?
- How will you use literacy as your personal pathway to freedom?

## Wrap-Up (10 minutes)

Once the students have completed their essays, revisit and discuss the essential questions:

- In what ways does literacy create pathways to freedom?
- What role does literacy play in social and political activism?
- What role does literacy play in your life?

Encourage the students to reference some of the points made in their essays as part of this discussion.

# As she sits down to write...:
## Using Primary Sources to Understand the Past[73]

### Noël M. Voltz

**Intended Audience:**

High school Social Studies

**Overview:**

This series of lessons helps students understand the importance of primary sources to the study of history. Utilizing an active learning approach, students will be introduced to primary sources and will begin the process of understanding how historians use primary source material to offer a more complete view of the past. Specifically, students will be able to explore the important role that primary sources play in the construction of any historical narrative by examining *Notes from a Colored Girl*.[74] In addition, through analyzing the Davis diaries, as well as constructing their own personal diaries, students will not only get a better understanding of how primary sources are created, but they will also explore what information different sources can hold, the potential limitations of any one source, as well as forging connections between their lives and the past. Ultimately, this lesson plan will encourage students to understand their role both as learners and creators of history, and through this process, they will learn to critically analyze both the histories that they read and also the materials they produce.

**Scope and Sequence:**

This series of lessons begins with introducing students to primary source documents. More specifically, they will learn what a primary source is and how they are created. After mastering this initial concept, students will use the pocket diaries of Emilie Davis, a free woman of color living in Civil War Philadelphia, as a lens to explore how primary sources are created, and read these sources with a critical eye for understanding and potential bias. *The lessons will culminate in a project in which the students produce their own primary source document in the form of a pocket diary, and also explore how primary sources can help historians and students make connections with the past.*

**National Standards for History**

Standard 3: Historical Thinking

- Consider multiple perspectives of various peoples in the past by demonstrating their differing motives, beliefs, interests, hopes, and fears.
- Draw comparisons across eras and regions in order to define enduring issues as well as large-scale or long-term developments that transcend regional and temporal boundaries
- Compare competing historical narratives

Standard 4: Historical Thinking

- Formulate historical questions from encounters with historical documents, eyewitness accounts, letters, diaries, artifacts, photos, historical sites, art, architecture, and other records from the past.
- Obtain historical data from a variety of sources, including: library and museum collections, historic sites, historical photos, journals, diaries, eyewitness accounts, newspapers, and the like; documentary films, oral testimony from living witnesses, censuses, tax records, city directories, statistical compilations, and economic indicators.
- Interrogate historical data by uncovering the social, political, and economic context in which it was created; testing the data source for its credibility, authority, authenticity, internal consistency and completeness; and detecting and evaluating bias, distortion, and propaganda by omission, suppression, or invention of facts.
- Identify the gaps in the available record and marshal contextual knowledge and perspectives of the time and place in order to elaborate imaginatively upon the evidence, fill in the gaps deductively, and construct a sound historical interpretation.

**Common Core State Standards in History/Social Studies**
- CCSS.ELA-LITERACY.RH.9-10.1. Cite specific textual evidence to support analysis of primary and secondary sources, attending to such features as the date and origin of the information.
- CCSS.ELA-LITERACY.RH.9-10.2. Determine the central ideas or information of a primary or secondary source; provide an accurate summary of how key events or ideas develop over the course of the text.
- CCSS.ELA-LITERACY.RH.9-10.9. Compare and contrast treatments of the same topic in several primary and secondary sources.
- CCSS.ELA-LITERACY.RH.11-12.1. Cite specific textual evidence to support analysis of primary and secondary sources, connecting insights gained from specific details to an understanding of the text as a whole.
- CCSS.ELA-LITERACY.RH.11-12.2. Determine the central ideas or information of a primary or secondary source; provide an accurate summary that makes clear the relationships among the key details and ideas.
- CCSS.ELA-LITERACY.RH.11-12.3. Evaluate various explanations for actions or events and determine which explanation best accord with textual evidence, acknowledging where the text leaves matters uncertain.

## Objectives
- Identify the differences between primary and secondary sources.
- Examine and evaluate primary sources for potential biases.
- Analyze primary sources to help students make connections to the past, present, and future.

## Essential Questions
- What are primary sources and how do they inform our understanding and interpretations of the past?

- What information can historians gather from primary sources? What are the potential limitations of primary sources?
- How can primary sources help students connect to the past?

## Resources for Teachers

- Library of Congress. "Using Primary Sources." Accessed March 27, 2014. http://www.loc.gov/teachers/usingprimarysources/
- Library of Congress. "Why Use Primary Sources." Accessed March 27, 2014. http://www.loc.gov/teachers/usingprimary-sources/whyuse.html
- National Archives. "History in the Raw." Accessed March 27, 2014. http://www.archives.gov/education/research/history-in-the-raw.html
- Vest, Kathleen. *Using Primary Sources in the Classroom: Examining Our Past, Understanding Our Present, Considering Our Future. Huntington Beach:* Shell Education, 2005.

# DAY ONE: *Introduction to Primary Sources*

**Preparation:**

Bring a few different examples of primary sources into the classroom. You can do this with physical items that you might have in your personal or school library (i.e. an old photo album, newspaper, journal, a map, a will, etc.), digitally with images of different types of primary sources, or both. If possible, try to include images of the Emile Davis pocket diary in your sample so that the students will already be introduced to the diary in passing.[75]

**Motivation** (10 minutes)

Tell students that they are going to spend the next week thinking about how history is created and more specifically, how and where historians get their information about the past.

To encourage active participation and to assess students' prior knowledge, ask students to brainstorm a list of documents/items that a historian might use in order to gain knowledge about the past. As students begin to share their ideas, list them on the board and place them into two categories (primary sources and secondary sources). This brainstorming session should generate a variety of ideas that might include items like "newspapers," "diaries," "maps," "books," "census," etc.

If students are having a hard time generating ideas, do a role-playing exercise in which you tell students to imagine that they are historians who want to write a history of the school. Help them to create a list of documents that they might use to construct this school history. Answers can include yearbooks, maps, a list of their teachers, report cards, class schedules, and sports trophies. Use this exercise as a springboard back to brainstorming a list of all of the different types of materials an historian can use to explore the past.

**Whole class: Mini-Lecture** (20 minutes)

Give a mini lecture about primary sources drawing on the brainstormed list, and explain to students that there are two categories of materials that historians use when examining the past: 1) primary sources, and 2) secondary sources. A primary source is an original first-hand testimony, document or record that was created during the time period that you are studying. Even more specifically, they are "materials produced by people or groups directly involved in the event or topic under consideration."[76] Primary sources come in many forms and can include: pamphlets, newspapers, magazines, diaries, artifacts—like clothing, furniture, jewelry, maps, paintings, cartoons, photographs, and government documents—codes of law, legal certificates, census records, and many more. As you explain what primary sources are, share your prepared examples.

After spending time clearly defining primary sources, also define what a secondary source is in order to make sure that students understand the difference. A secondary source uses primary sources to create an interpretation of the past. Thus, historians produce secondary sources because they use primary sources to explain what occurred in a particular time period. An example of a secondary source is a textbook. Explain that this week we will be focusing on primary sources—what are they, where they come from, what this information can they tell us about the past, and how historians use these sources.

Follow your mini-lecture with a short "check-in assessment" and ask them to re-explain what a primary source is in order to verify that they have understood the concepts you presented.

Then ask your students to return to the brainstormed list and add any other types of sources that they might not have thought of originally. If needed, guide them through this process. In the end you should have sources that fall into all of the following categories:
- Printed Materials: magazines, pamphlets, newspapers, almanacs, advertisements, etc.
- Manuscript sources: diaries, journals, letters, speeches, etc.
- Artifacts: furniture, clothing, jewelry, weaponry, instruments, tools, etc.

- Visual: paintings, maps, photographs, prints, cartoons, etc.
- Audio: oral history, music, etc.
- Legal: laws, census records, certificates of marriage, birth, property ownership, or death, etc.

Once it is clear that students have a solid understanding of what primary sources are, introduce the concept that every primary source can tell us about the past but they do so in different ways. Using the brainstormed list, ask students to think about the different types of information that they might be able to get from an artifact, a map, a newspaper, and a diary.

## Activity: Small Group (15 minutes)

Break students into four (or more if necessary) small groups and assign each group a particular source (i.e. a piece of clothing, a map, a newspaper, a diary, etc.) and have them discuss together what information that that source might tell a historian.

## Wrap-Up (10 minutes)

Conclude class with a quick overview of primary sources and introduce the topic for next class, which is going to be exploring how primary sources are created.

## DAY TWO: Telling Your Story: Exploring How a Primary Source is Created

**Motivation** (15 minutes)

Open class with a review of what they learned the day before. To help with this review process tell students to pretend that they are historians in the year 2120 and tell them to image that they came across a technological artifact from the past. Have your students pretend that this is the only piece of information that they have found about life in 2014.

Choose a "technological artifact" that is currently trendy like: a cell phone, a Facebook page, an Instagram page, a twitter feed, a newspaper, or a popular television show.

Have a class discussion about what that particular item might tell a historian about today's society. Push students to think about how much material they can learn from a single item, but also about how that item does not tell the whole story. Tell them that this last point will be discussed further in a few days.

Now that you have student's thinking about primary sources, ask them to talk about how these sources were created and their intended audience. For example, depending on your previous activity, this might lead to a discussion about how who creates a Facebook profile, what information they include on their profile, and who is the audience. Use this discussion as a springboard into a mini-lecture on the creation of primary sources

**Whole Class: Mini Lecture** (15 minutes)

Give a mini-lecture in which you discuss how and why primary sources were originally created highlighting the difference between public and private documents.

You should also explore why people choose to document what they do. Introduce Emilie Davis and her pocket diaries to the class and use them as you central example primary source.

For instance, you might discuss that her diaries were her private records, spaces in which she documented her movements.

You could also discuss when she chose to write and when she stopped writing her diaries (tell students for the purposes of this discussion, they are going to assume that she stopped writing and not that her later writings have yet to be discovered).[77]

Encourage students to begin to think about why and what gets recorded and also the implications of these facts. As well, help students to consider how audience might impact what is contained in any particular source.

**Activity: Small Group** (15 minutes)

Break students back into the small groups that they were in the day before and have them re-examine the source that they were assigned.

Have the students discuss and write down answers to the follow questions: What is the source? Who wrote it? What is the document about? What information might a historian be able to glean from the item/document? Who was its intended audience? Is it a public or private source? How might the audience impact the information included in the source?

If you have Internet access, tell the groups to research the author and the document to provide some background information.

Time permitting, have students present their information to the class. If not, have them turn in the group notes from the discussion for you to examine.

**Wrap-Up** (5 minutes)

Encourage students to continue to think about how and why documents are created and how this information could impact their content. Explain that tomorrow they will be examining Emilie's diary to explore what information is discussed in a private source.

**Homework** (10 minutes)

Tell students that for the next few days, they will keep a "pocket diary." Explain to students that they should write in their diary everyday for the remaining duration of the lesson plan series (approximately 5 entries). A "sample" diary worksheet is included with this lesson plan. Each day they should write a minimum of 40 words (similar in length to Emile's diary entries) in which they account their lives for that particular day. You might suggest the following topics: food they ate, where they went that day, what they learned in school, who they talked to or ate lunch with, what were the topics of conversation, what activities did they do for fun after school, what were some of their happy/sad/ nervous /excited/ angry moment, something funny that happened, the news, the weather, etc. Make sure to emphasize that each diary will be different and that they should choose to write on whatever part of their life feels important to them. They should bring this diary with them to class each day.

*Important note: Make sure that students understand that what they write about will only be read by the teacher and will not be discussed in class unless they choose to share their writing but that there will be one day when they will be required to share a few examples (of their choosing) from their diary with the class.*

# DAY THREE: *"When and Where I Enter" Reading and Understanding Primary Sources*[78]

**Motivation** (15 minutes)

Open class by giving a presentation about Emilie Davis—her life as a free woman of color, a seamstress and a domestic, and her world in Civil War Philadelphia. Also, introduce the people in her world. It might be useful to include images of a family tree to help students better visualize the material. Explain that much of the information that historians know about her has come from using her pocket diaries to reconstruct a narrative about her life. This reconstruction is then used to find her (or events or people that she mentioned) in other primary sources, including the U.S. Census, church records, and club notes. Time permitting, students can go through the "Who's Who" section of *Notes from a Colored Girl* and create a family tree.

Have students brainstorm what kinds of topics they think she might have included in her diaries. If they need prompting, ask them to think about the topics they wrote about in their diary the past evening.

**Small Group Work** (20 minutes)

Break students into 5 groups and assign each group a portion of reading from Ch. 6 of Whitehead's *Notes from a Colored Girl.* The portions are: 1)"I have bin buisy with my dress," 2) "I went to the party and enjoyed myself nicely," 3) "Nellie and I, little Frenchy," 4) "I do not know how I could get along without him," and 5) "Concerning the several deaths."

Have the groups read the material out loud together looking for information about Emilie's life—or what she chose to write about. Have groups prepare a short creative presentation of the material from the diary that they learned about. For example, students assigned to the section "Concerning the several deaths" might draft a fictitious letter from

Emilie to "the girls" in which she is discussing how sad she is about all of the deaths in her family. The goal of these presentations is for students to share with the class one particular facet of Emilie's life that she chose to write about in her diary.

**Presentation and Class Discussion** (20 minutes)

Have groups present their creative work to the class. Also, have them provide a short summary of the material that they read about.

After students have completed their presentations discuss the materials that Emilie included in her diary and also how Whitehead was able to take short diary entries to create snapshots from Emilie's life.

**Wrap-Up** (5 minutes)

Conclude the day by explaining how important primary sources are to understanding the past and highlight the fact that primary sources can tell historians so much about the lives of their subjects. Weave excerpts from Emilie's diary throughout this wrap up. End this overview by making the point that while primary sources can provide a lot of information about the past, they are also limited in their scope and so it is important to also understand their limitations.

**Homework:**

Have students continue to work on their diaries.

# DAY FOUR: *"Where Yours Ends and Mine Begins"*
## *The Limitations of Primary Sources*

**Preparation:**

Bring in readable copies of the Philadelphia Inquirer newspaper from a single day that corresponds with a diary entry in Emile's pocket diary.[79] For example, you could use Monday March 2nd, 1863. Also bring in copies of the diary entry from the same day (with translation if needed).[80] You might need to include a short introductory paragraph with the diary entry to give it some context of that day's entry.[81]

**Motivation** (10 minutes)

Review with students all of the information that a primary source, like Emile's diary can tell us about life in Civil War Philadelphia for a free woman of color. After students have generated a list of ideas, introduce the concept that primary sources have limitations and ask students to brainstorm what some of those limitations might be.

**Mini-Lecture** (15 minutes)

Segue your brainstorming activity into a mini-lecture on the potential limitations of primary sources.[82] You should include the following points in your lecture:

- A primary source is only telling one point of view;
- The primary source is likely to contain bias;
- The producer of the item/document controls what is presented;
- Many primary sources are lost to time (i.e. records are lost) and so historians only have limited materials to use when constructing the past; and,
- The limitations of contextual factors (i.e. literacy among your subjects, whether something was valued in society or not, etc.).

To help students understand, use the critiques of the WPA slave narratives outlined in *Notes from a Colored Girl*.[83]

Have students brainstorm the potential limitations of Emilie's pocket diaries.

**Primary Source Exploration** (15 minutes)

Open the activity by explaining to students that they are going to be reading a newspaper from Philadelphia and the corresponding day's diary entry of Emilie (who lived in Philadelphia). The purpose of this exercise is to explore how sources that can functionally be about the "same topic"—in this case, life in Civil War Philadelphia—can tell very different stories.

Break students into groups of two and give each group a section of the newspaper and a copy of the diary excerpt. Have each partnership read the newspaper clipping together and write a few sentences describing its contents. The students should also write a short summary of the diary entry. Once they have completed these summaries have them discuss if they can see any potential overlaps between the two documents.

**Class Discussion** (15 minutes)

Once students have examined their documents, bring the class together for a discussion on the limitations of individual sources. Use these questions to guide your discussion:

- What was the focus of the diary entry? What was the focus of the newspaper?
- What happened on [insert document date], that was important to Emilie? What was important to the newspaper writers?
- Did you find any potential overlap between the newspaper and the diary entry? Explain your findings.
- If the two documents seemed very disconnected, how is it possible that they were both written on the same day, about life in the same city, and yet there are no similarities? In other words, why are these sources so different?
- Which source do you think is more "accurate"? Why?
- What potential biases exist in each source?
- If you were a historian of Civil War Philadelphia, which source(s)

would you use and why?

- How might using both sources provide a more complete understanding of the past?

**Wrap-Up** (10 minutes)

To conclude class, remind students of the activity that they did a few
days before when they imagined that they were historians in the future
who found a "technological artifact" (i.e. a person's twitter feed or a TV
show) from 2014.

Have students think about how limited this single source actually is.
Emphasize the fact that historians have to be careful when using primary
sources to ensure that they are telling a complete story and not just one
viewpoint that is likely biased in one way or another.

End class with a re-cap of your mini lecture emphasizing the importance that historians understand the limitations of any one primary
source.

**Homework**

Have students continue to work on their diaries and remind them to
bring their diaries to the next class session

# DAY FIVE: Using Primary Sources to Connect the Past and the Present

**Motivation** (10 minutes)

Open class with a review of material (i.e. the strengths and limitations of primary sources) from the previous two days. Prepare students to think more about why and how historians use primary sources.

**Reflection Essay** (30 minutes)

Explain to students that they are going to write a reflective essay to synthesize the learning activities over the past few days.

Write the following questions on the board and give the students time to discuss and reflect on them: Why are primary sources important? What can they tell us about history? In what ways is your life similar or different to Emilie Davis's life based on your knowledge of her diary and the journal you have been keeping for the past week?

**Class Discussion** (15 minutes)

Once students have completed their reflection paper. Facilitate a classroom discussion about primary sources and how they help create connections to the past. Through this discussion, helps students to draw connections between their lives and Emilie's life. The following is a list of potential discussion questions:
- In what ways is your life similar to Emile's? How are they different? Are there things that Emile does that you do in your daily life?
- Considering what we have learned about Emilie's life, what appears to be important to her? Looking at your diary, what is important for you?
- What are primary sources and how do they inform our understandings and interpretations of the past?
- What information can historians gather from primary sources?

What are the potential limitations of primary sources?

• How can primary sources help students connect to the past?

**Wrap-Up** (5 minutes)

As a final note, you might encourage your students to continue writing in their diary explaining to them that their writing might eventually be found, like Emile's pocket diaries, and that thus, they are creating a primary source that historians might be able to use in the future to learn about life in the early 2000s.

_____

(Name)

Pocket Diary for _____

(Month and Year)

*"I write; therefore, I exist and, therefore, I am."*

Date:_____

_____
_____
_____
_____
_____
_____
_____
_____
_____
_____
_____
_____
_____
_____
_____
_____
_____
_____
_____
_____
_____
_____

# Section II

# The Road to Freedom

*This section contains five lesson plan sets that knit together stories that explore the different ways that Emilie Frances Davis and the free black community explored and claimed political, social, and economic freedom.*

# A Black Feminist Interpretation: Reading Life, Pedagogy, and Emilie

**Conra D. Gist**

Reading life through the lens of black feminism offers the reader an analytical framework for interpreting the social world. Disturbing images and treatment of black women can be seen as a set of social scripts that are the "legacy of racism, sexism, class exploitation, and heterosexism that assign categories of superiority and inferiority."[84] In this sense, black feminism functions as a critical social theory that helps readers of the social world understand how black women can be marginalized through institutional structures and practices, social norms, and ideological elitism. A critical consciousness of the patterns of inequality facilitates a process in which new social narratives of justice can be written to eliminate these practices. To consider how reading life in black feminism can allow the reader to understand the ways in which institutional structures and individual practices can conspire to privilege certain groups, let's explore a scenario that describes a person who does not look through the scope of black feminism while pursuing her education. For example, imagine the person is a young black girl from a working class background in the United States. This particular girl reads the social world as a competitive arena where society's winners and losers are determined based on the quality of an individual's effort. She reasons that if her actions mirror hard working winners, then she will be academically successful. Her theory of achievement is individuals can achieve their dreams through dedication and hard work. At first glance this appears to be a logical approach to explaining her social world. Now suppose she works hard but she does not achieve her dream, for example, of college acceptance at an elite university. How might she understand this outcome?

Based on her individual theory of achievement, it is likely that she will seek to understand how her behavior caused the outcome. Although taking personal responsibility is in some sense a healthy adaptive approach, it will undoubtedly yield an incomplete understanding of her rejection letters if it is not married with systemic and social analysis. Without a deeper analysis she is not likely to consider how her educational context is rooted in policy and practices that have evolved out of a system of institutional racism, classism, and sexism that invariably leads to various scenarios like the tracking of students of color from low income and working class communities into high schools with the least experienced and lowest paid teachers; school systems failing to provide AP course options in urban schools that could strengthen college applications; having limited local access to SAT prep training and arts related extra-curricular activities; high school counselors who fail to advise girls to take advanced STEM courses; and teachers who write superior letters of recommendation based on a student's social and economic situation and not their grades. An understanding of the complex educational system would give her a more robust picture of how she is situated in a school structure that does not only reward effort, but also assigns unmerited power and privilege based on various social categories.

Without this view, she may think, "If only I had talked to other teachers, or researched additional leadership opportunities. If only I were smarter. If only." Furthermore, if this young black girl views her life chances and opportunities solely as a product of personal effort and ability, how might she manage her psychological and emotional health when she experiences setbacks? The process of personal blaming can foster a dangerous state of inferiority. She may analyze her defeats as an accurate measure of her value, competence, and belonging in society and believe if only she could fix herself, her life would (could) be better. In her read of the world "winning" does not require incorporating a collective identity of critique, struggle, and empowerment, such as black feminism. She does not have a community of "sisters" to affirm her experiences and help her make meaning of an inequitable schooling system. In this example the young black girl's de-raced, de-gendered, and de-classed individualistic theory of achievement is no match for the inequitable structures and practices of the education system. She can still continue the uphill battle of applying her individualistic theory of achievement to realize her dreams. It is just that her way forward puts her at risk of repeated disappointment that could feed an internalized inferiority if her individual theory does not work in tandem with a critical set of knowledge, tools, and strategies such as: knowledge of how structures, practices, and ideologies can work to unequally disadvantage certain groups of people; affirmation and participation in a beloved community that acts as a tool and shield to help her recover and continue her educational pursuits; and a framework for identifying and addressing problems that is grounded in an ongoing process of critical analysis and action in an effort to live a self-defined and self-determined life.

Since young black girls are an eclectic and diverse group, this means they are differently positioned in an interlocking system of power relations based on various social categories. Therefore, they can and do read society through various and competing lenses other than black feminism. And even girls who are fluent readers of black feminism in the social world do not necessarily articulate similar interpretations. But for those young black girls without clearly articulated social theories but the passion and faith to fight for a better world, or innocent perceptions of a just world that equally rewards effort, reading life with a black feminist lens can act as armor and weapon in a complex and at times dangerous world. Looking through a black feminist lens, the often hidden from view raced, gendered, and classed minefields that can kill her dreams are clearly seen. Her ability to read the systemic dangers in her social world allows her to take strategic steps towards a free and self-determined life.

### Transforming a Dangerous World in the Classroom

Collins argues that "Black feminist thought is but one expression of many self-defined standpoints produced by people whose location within intersecting power relations of race, class, gender, sexuality, age, and religion mandate that they glorify their respective emperors."[85] The term emperor refers to "powerful groups and their interests" and the structures and practices that uphold and sustain their interests. The standpoints are meant to "challenge dominant knowledge that upholds unjust social inequalities."[86] Given the emancipatory tenor of black feminism, it can be an insightful and instructive framework for teachers to resist reproducing inequality in the context of their classroom. Black feminism, applied as a critical pedagogic lens, can be utilized to read the classroom as a place and space for personal and collective transformation. From this interpretation of black feminism, I argue black feminist critical pedagogy can be positioned to equip students to transgress teaching and learning inequities in at least four ways.

First, black feminist critical pedagogy can honor and build upon the intrinsic value of students by viewing their lived experiences as worthy sites of intellectual investigation. There is an explicit emphasis on supporting and guiding students who are often unjustly marginalized in schools. For example, when the inherent value and worth of black girls is overlooked in classrooms in comparison to other groups, a critical consciousness of historical, structural, and cultural norms of inequality provide a framework of analysis for black feminist critical pedagogues to understand the root causes of differential treatment and challenge inequitable institutional practices. Second, black feminist critical pedagogy is conceptually situated to view students as constructors of deep understandings and generators of knowledge. Black feminism is a critical knowledge project that generates knowledge and creates theories that allow for analysis, critique, and evaluation of how black women are situated as social agents in society.[87] This knowledge project is grounded in a black feminist perspective that challenges the intellectual repression of social groups who do not mimic but instead refute dominant views and perspectives on society. The commitment to the unequivocal value of all students as constructors and generators of knowledge is not simply an intellectual exercise, but rather a process in which students develop a set of critical skills that enable them to honor and transform themselves and society by developing fresh and just ways of viewing and experiencing the world.

Also, the positioning of students as constructors instead of reproducers of knowledge necessitates the ability to critically think about texts. Black feminist critical pedagogy challenges students not to readily accept all texts as authoritative sources, but instead to problematize and question them as contestable knowledge sources. Taking this view can work to shift how students view themselves as thinkers and knowledge generators in the context of the classroom, and serve as a catalyst to challenge students to claim, name, and write their own stories, theories, and policies. Black feminist pedagogy can also be utilized to help students develop fluency in reading the social world from multiple standpoints such as race, class, gender, sexuality, age, and nationality. Looking through the lenses of a multiplicity of positionalities unsettles the notion of one correct view of society and invites students to question taken for granted views of the social world. In this sense, black feminist critical pedagogy can also decenter dominant pedagogical and epistemological views expressed in texts, lesson plans, assessments, and instructional strategies by repositioning these mandated texts and instructional practices alongside alternative pedagogies that express diverse ways of viewing knowledge and seeing the world.

Finally, black feminist critical pedagogy must produce a change for good in the classroom. The ability of this pedagogical stance to improve the life chances and opportunities for marginalized student groups, and black girls and women in particular, is the measure of its value as a social justice project in the classroom.[88] Black feminism in the U.S. is grounded in a history of unrelenting commitment to resist and overcome inequality. The lives of Ella Baker and Septima Clark, for example, are not simply evoked by black feminists to convey nostalgic stories of the past when these black women invested their lives in the project of social justice. Rather, their lives as texts are read as active sites of investigation because they provide clues and strategies for how to press forward with what at times may feel like the unbearable work of justice. The ways in which black women describe transgressing the challenges of their social world in autobiographies, testimonies, narratives, and diaries can function as textual compass points when despair and fatigue cause teachers to lose their sense of critical pedagogical direction in the classroom. Taken as a whole, black feminism, read as critical pedagogic practice, enables teachers and students to read a dangerous set of social inequalities and cultivate empowering and effective strategies for transformative learning possibilities in and outside of the classroom.

## Reading Emilie Frances Davis

Teachers and students can concretely practice reading the world with a black feminist lens by critically reading diverse texts across various mediums and disciplines. For instance, Whitehead's *Notes from a Colored Girl: The Civil War Pocket Diaries of Emilie Frances Davis* can serve as an instructive site of black feminist textual investigation because it contributes to the critical knowledge project advanced by black women. Three features serve as evidence that Whitehead is contributing to the critical knowledge work of black women: 1) the text content describes the process of finding, recovering, and transcribing a three-year period of a black woman's life during the Civil War; 2) Whitehead applies race and gender as lenses of historical analysis and interpretation; and 3) Whitehead historically situates herself as part of ongoing justice efforts on the part of black feminists and activists.

In *Notes*, Whitehead delineates a narrative that grapples with the complexity of a free black woman's lived experience during the Civil War. Students have the opportunity to see how a historian takes a critical perspective to resurrect a black woman's writing from a time period when black women's writing was limited and repressed. In this sense, teachers and students can see how Whitehead is generating knowledge about the black female experience by developing and situating the narrative as part of a limited cannon of detailed personal accounts that describe the lives of everyday free black women during the Civil War. Additionally, by transcribing and reconstructing the life of Emilie Frances Davis, Whitehead provides an opportunity for readers to position Notes alongside other texts and engage in comparative analysis and interpretation that explores, for instance, the history of black Philadelphians and/or the diverse experiences of black free women during the Civil War.

Whitehead also situates herself and her work within a history of black activists and scholars. She views herself as standing on the shoulders of other activists, and in doing so, continues the ongoing struggle to center instead of marginalize the black female experience in history. In other words, the project of documenting black women's testimonies and narratives has historically acted as a form of critical knowledge activism that is committed to writing the often excluded lives of black women in to existence.[89] In the spirit of writing activism, Whitehead actively explores the implications of race and gender in this process by using a black feminist herstorical lens to analyze Emilie's life in the pocket diaries. Race and gender is key to understanding Emilie's life choices, experiences, and the types of opportunity she was afforded. Therefore, reading the life of Emile Frances Davis permits readers to deepen their critical consciousness of social inequality in a historical context while simultaneously seeing the text as part of an ongoing effort to generate critical knowledge about the lives of black women.

Finally, reading the life of Emilie offers a rich opportunity for teachers and students to engage in countless critical thinking questions using a black feminist lens, such as: *What were the dominant social scripts about black women during the Civil War? How do Emilie's diaries, as a public record, challenge or affirm the social scripts and narratives written about black women during the Civil War? Although Emilie enjoyed certain liberties as a free woman, in what ways was she still unsafe as a black woman living in the Philadelphia? How did racial, gender, and economic inequality work through institutional structures and social practices in Philadelphia during this time period? How might the reconstructed life of Emilie Frances Davis be different if it were written from the gaze of a white male perspective in contrast to a black female perspective? In what ways might Whitehead be working to disrupt the collective imagination about black women during the Civil War? How does Emilie's life unsettle contemporary understandings of black women as intellectuals during the latter part of the nineteenth-century? How is shame experienced in raced, classed, and gendered ways in Emilie's pocket diaries? How did power relations between men and women, and between women, shape Emilie's lived experiences? How, if at all, does Emilie express a sense of cognitive dissonance between her life as a free woman and the lives of enslaved women during that time period? How does Emilie read and understand how inequality shapes her life? How, if at all, does she analyze social problems and take action? How did Emilie's social community help her navigate obstacles?* By no means does this reflect an exhaustive list of questions about the life of Emilie, but rather the questions are an attempt to offer a sense of how readers can possibly wear black feminist lenses to begin contemplating the story of her life during the Civil War.

### Reading for freedom

Wearing a black feminist lens to read life, pedagogy, and Emilie reveals an unrelenting commitment to critique and act in ways that dismantle barriers and create opportunities for black women to live free and self-determined lives.  In this sense, black feminism can also be read as an intellectual activism that seeks to disrupt social hierarchies through the power of ideas.[90] hooks posits, "Critical pedagogy, the sharing of information and knowledge by black women with Black women, is crucial for the development of radical black female subjectivity (not because Black women can only learn from one another, but because the circumstances of racism, sexism, and class exploitation ensure that other groups will not necessarily seek to further their self-determination)."[91] Whitehead illustrates this practice in her reconstruction of Emilie Frances Davis because she utilizes the experiential knowledge noted in Emilie's pocket diaries to craft a revealing and complex narrative about a black woman's experience during the Civil War.  In doing so, it allows the reader to study a set of critical questions that he or she may not have otherwise considered when reading a traditional U.S. history textbook that may misrepresent or leave out Black women. The text also provides an opportunity for teachers and students to ruminate on the production of historical knowledge—What is the process by which the historian identifies reliable sources of evidence and makes knowledge claims? How does the historian's social positionality influence analysis and interpretation? Who benefits from the views of knowledge expressed by the historian? How does the knowledge set work to affirm or challenge power relations in society?

If a black feminist pedagogue required that the young black girl at the beginning of this essay read *Notes from a Colored Girl: The Civil War Pocket Diaries of Emilie Frances Davis*, she would be reading a critical knowledge project launched by a black feminist who is building on the activist work of previous generations of black women as a form of intellectual activism. She would be reading a journey of freedom penned at the dawn of the Emancipation Proclamation, and carried on in the lives of black women who lived for justice and encouraged souls that would shape the lived experience of Whitehead during the latter part of the twentieth century. She would read how this legacy positioned Whitehead to evolve as a black feminist scholar who would reconstruct the life of Emilie Frances Davis over 150 years later. She may even see that the politics of black feminist identity do not simply aspire for individual gain. A close reading through the language of black feminism would reveal a collective identity working to create a more humane and just world for families and communities. She may even read with a desire and anticipation for clues to help her understand how she, as a black girl, is positioned as a herstorical and social agent in society. In an unassuming way, this young black girl may even begin to read the social world as an emergent reader of black feminism. Her fluency can be further nurtured by black feminist pedagogy in the classroom. But ultimately, her desire to master the language may depend on black feminism's utility and transformative power as she navigates her complex and at times dangerous social world.

# Using A Black Feminist Interpretation to Examine Emilie's Diaries

## Conra D. Gist

**Intended Audience:**
11th and 12th graders

**Overview:**

Whitehead's *Notes from a Colored Girl* is a rich and layered text that describes the life of a free black woman during the Civil War through a herstorical analysis of her diaries. The text also explains the journey of a historian who uses a black feminist lens to begin an in depth journey of researching, transcribing, and ultimately creating a book on the life of Emilie Frances Davis. Although there are numerous areas of study to explore as it relates to Whitehead's depiction of Emilie's life, this lesson plan set examines the idea of black feminism as a lens that can be used for interpreting Notes as well as other texts such as essays, articles, video clips, and music lyrics. Since these lessons will only take place over the course of five brief lessons, students are not expected to be black feminist experts at the end of the lesson series. However, students will develop a novice level of understanding related to black feminism by synthesizing themes across texts and reflecting on black feminism as a system of thought for reading texts and understanding the social world.

**Scope and Sequence:**

This lesson plan set aims to explore black feminism by reading, analyzing, and reflecting on a series of texts. Specifically, the lesson plan set will begin by having students read the "Black Feminist Interpretation" essay and explore and reflect on the arguments made about black feminism. Next, students will use a black feminist lens to read sections of Notes from a Colored Girl and contemplate various interpretations of the text.

Students will also use a black feminist lens to analyze recent videos of speeches, mini-documentaries, and music lyrics. Finally, the lesson plan set will conclude by asking students to complete a group performance task in which they develop a presentation to a school board on the need to include the study of black feminism in the school curriculum. Students will draw from the texts explored in previous lessons, in particular Notes, to support claims and address counterclaims about black feminism.

**Preparation notes:**

This lesson plan set is developed for students who have extensive experience working in groups, leading and participating in discussion, and critiquing texts. Expectations and accountability structures for listening, participating, and contributing to groups should be established prior to the beginning of this lesson plan set. Also, although this lesson plan set is written to provide student's with foundational exposure and mean making experiences in black feminism as a system of thought for reading texts and the social world, students will need some basic understanding of the constructs of race and gender, for example, to grapple with the content in a meaningful manner.

**Common Core ELA and Literacy Standards in Social Studies[92]**

- CCSS.ELA-Literacy.RI.11-12.1. Cite strong and thorough textual evidence to support analysis of what the text says explicitly as well as inferences drawn from the text, including determining where the text leaves matters uncertain.
- CSSS.ELA-Literacy.RI.11-12.7. Integrate and evaluate multiple sources of information presented in different media or formats (e.g., visually, quantitatively) as well as in words in order to address a question or solve a problem.
- CSSS.ELA-Literacy.RI.11-12. Evaluate various explanations for actions or events and determine which explanation best accords with textual evidence, acknowledging where the text leaves matters uncertain.
- CCSS.ELA-Literacy.W.11-12.1. Write arguments to support

claims in an analysis of substantive topics or texts, using valid reasoning and relevant and sufficient evidence.

- CSSS.ELA-Literacy.SL.11-12.1.b. Work with peers to promote civil, democratic discussions and decision-making, set clear goals and deadlines, and establish individual roles as needed.
- CCSS.ELA-Literacy.SL.11-12.4. Present information, findings, and supporting evidence, conveying a clear and distinct perspective, such that listeners can follow the line of reasoning, alternative or opposing perspectives are addressed, and the organization, development, substance, and style are appropriate to purpose, audience, and a range of formal and informal tasks.
- CCSS.ELA-Literacy.SL.11-12.5. Make strategic use of digital media (e.g., textual, graphical, audio, visual, and interactive elements) in presentations to enhance understanding of findings, reasoning, and evidence and to add interest.
- CCSS.ELA-Literacy.SL.11-12.6. Adapt speech to a variety of contexts and tasks, demonstrating a command of formal English when indicated or appropriate.
- CCSS.ELA-Literacy.RH.11-12.1. Cite specific textual evidence to support analysis of primary and secondary sources, connecting insights gained from specific details to an understanding of the text as a whole.
- CCSS.ELA-Literacy.RH.11-12.2. Determine the central ideas or information of a primary or secondary source; provide an accurate summary that makes clear the relationships among the key details and ideas.
- CCSS.ELA.Literacy.RH.11-12.3. Evaluate various explanations for actions or events and determine which explanation best accords with textual evidence, acknowledging where the text leaves matters uncertain.

## Objectives

- Engage in textual analysis of articles, essays, video clips, and music lyrics to comprehend various black feminist perspectives.

- Examine primary sources to draw conclusions about the author's point of view.
- Discuss issues related to black feminist perspectives.
- Construct understandings of black feminism by synthesizing ideas across texts.
- Collaborate in groups to plan and design a persuasive presentation on black feminism.
- Write reflections and arguments related to the study of black feminism.

## Essential Questions
- What is black feminism? Why is it an important area of study?
- How can a black feminist lens be used to critically read the social world? Texts?
- What core themes emerge across black feminist perspectives?

# DAY ONE: *Reading black feminism*

**Overview** (10 minutes)

Explain to students that they will be exploring a system of ideas called black feminism through the reading and analysis of a series of texts over the next five lessons. Be sure to note that the lesson plans will culminate in a performance task presentation in which they will have to discuss, critique, and defend the utility of black feminism as an area of study in the school curriculum.

Tell students that the overarching question for today's lesson is: what is black feminism? To activate student schema, ask students to take a moment and write a quick 2-minute response to the question. Allow a few students to share their responses.

**Independent reading** (30 minutes)

As an initial step to explore an author's view of black feminism, tell students they will read "A Black Feminist Interpretation: Reading Life, Pedagogy, and Emilie." Explain to students that part of their work as critical readers of text is to not automatically assume the authority of text, but rather to read closely the claims made by the author and consider the evidence (or lack thereof) used by the author to support claims. To practice this approach, tell students they should keep the following questions in mind when reading the essay:

- How does the author define black feminism?
- According to the author, how can black feminism be used to read life?
- What sources, evidence or examples does the author use the support her claims about black feminism?
- What parts of her argument do you find most compelling? Why? What claims would you challenge? Why?
- What vocabulary did you find confusing or difficult to under-

stand? How did you go about making inferences related to the meaning of unfamiliar words?

**Small Group discussion** (20 minutes)

Explain to students that they will be organized in learning teams to complete several activities and tasks over the next couple of lessons. Note: Teams can be organized based on student interests, learning styles, and/ or readiness levels. The size of the group will vary based on time, but in general, 3-5 students can be assigned to each group.

Have students convene in their assigned groups. Assign one or more questions from the list in step 3 to each group and ask students to discuss their responses with their group members. Tell students that one group member will take notes on the discussion, another member will facilitate discussion, and another member will write/draw a visual representation on paper of the group's answer to the question(s) as well as any other pertinent ideas that emerge from the group discussion. As time winds down have each group finalize their visual presentation on chart paper and post the charts in designated areas in the classroom.

**Chart Walk & Talk** (15 minutes)

Allow time for students to peruse the charts posted throughout the classroom and reflect on the comments made by their classmates. Encourage students to discuss their observations with one another when reading and reflecting on each chart posted.

**Closure** (10 minutes)

After students have had time to read their peers' responses and reflect on their  interpretations of the text, bring the whole class together to revisit the question: What is black feminism? As time permits allow students to share their answer to this question based on their interpretation of the essay.

**Evaluation** (5 minutes)

Have students return to the initial quick write reflection they wrote on black feminism, and based on the reading and class discussion, write their emerging understanding of black feminism in their own words. Create a comparative exit slip asking the students "What is black feminism?" and make observations based on students' responses to the question. Consider how you may need to adjust or revisit key ideas in the next lesson.

**Homework**

Tell students that there are multiple views on black feminism and one of the ways they will continue to explore various perspectives is that they will be assigned articles for homework to continue expanding their understanding of black feminism. As a discussion device for the next lesson, students will keep a comparative organizer note-taking template on the articles read to assist with examining themes across texts and jog their memory for discussion on the following day. Explain to students that they are to come to class prepared to discuss the assigned texts over the next two lessons. Depending on students' readiness level adjustments to assigned readings are likely necessary.

**Possible readings**[93]
Lesson #1: Patricia Hill Collins
Lesson #2: bell hooks

**Sample Note-taking Template** (the chart should be organized in such a way that it provides a visual of how the questions extend across the text)
*Author: Patricia Hill Collins*

*1. How does the author define black feminism?*

*2. What sources, evidence or examples does the author use the support her claims about black feminism?*

*3. Based on your reading of the article, what new ideas, questions, or comments do you have?*

*Author: bell hooks*

*1. How does the author define black feminism?*

*2. What sources, evidence or examples does the author use the support her claims about black feminism?*

*3. Based on your reading of the article, what new ideas, questions, or comments do you have?*

# DAY TWO: *Reading Emilie—Looking through a black feminist lens*

**Warm-Up** (10 minutes)

Ask students to take out their comparative organizer based on the assigned reading for homework and meet in groups to discuss how the idea of black feminism was defined and consider similarities and differences between the previous day's essays.

**Shared Reading** (15 minutes)

Tell students that wearing a black feminist lens can enable them to see the social world in ways that may have been previously invisible or incomprehensible. Specifically, explain to students that a black feminist lens can be used to critically read texts.

Revisit the Black Feminist Interpretation essay and conduct a shared reading of the first three paragraphs in the section titled "Reading Emilie." Consider questions that you may want to pose to students based on their exit slip responses from the previous lesson. Be sure to explore how a black feminist lens is being used to view and interpret the significance of *Notes* in this passage.

**Independent reading** (20 minutes)

Instead of simply taking the author's view of Emilie in the Black Feminist Interpretation essay, students will be assigned sections of *Notes* (e.g., xiv, pages 4 and 5, and sections from chapter 5) to making meaning of Whitehead's view of herself as a forensic herstorical investigator who uses a black feminist lens. Have students distill their thinking as they read by underlining evidence in the texts, questioning claims, and drawing inferences and conclusions based on their interpretations of the text. In particular, they should read thinking about how they would answer the following question: How did Whitehead use this black feminist lens to help her write *Notes*?[100]

**Small group and Class Discussion** (15 minutes)

Have students meet in their group to discuss observations made during their independent reading. In particular, have the group develop a response to the question regarding the ways in which Whitehead used a black feminist lens in her analysis and writing of Emilie. If time allows, have groups share their response to the question and be sure they support their claims with evidence from the text.

**Closure** (10 minutes)

Wrap-up the lesson discussion by asking students how they think they used a black feminist lens to critically read sections from *Notes* and allow time for responses. Return to the last paragraph of the "Reading Emilie" section of the essay and tell students that the author is suggesting that addressing issues related to race, class, and gender are essential to the freedom and self-determination of black women.

**Evaluation** (10 minutes)

Have students independently read the last paragraph of the "Reading Emilie" section and answer the following questions on an exit slip: Based on the questions listed by the author, what issues and concerns appear to be particularly relevant to black feminism? Based on assigned readings, class discussion, or personal experiences, are the author's questions useful for reading Emilie with a black feminist lens? Why or why not? Based on student responses, consider how you may need to adjust or revisit key ideas in the next lesson.

**Homework**

Tell students to read the next assigned article on black feminism (e.g., bell hooks) and complete the note-taking template. Also, ask students to read Emilie's diary entries from 1863 (chapter 1).[101]

# DAY THREE: Reading Emilie: Was she a feminist?

**Warm-Up** (10 minutes)

Ask students to take out their comparative organizer based on the assigned reading for homework and meet in groups to discuss how the idea of black feminism was defined and consider similarities and differences between the previous readings and discussion.

**Class Discussion** (45 minutes)

Bring the class together and explain that today they will be engaged in a discussion about Emilie's diary entries and the readings on black feminism they have read thus far. To start the discussion, ask students to reflect back on the diary entries they were assigned to read and consider raising the following questions: How would you describe Emilie's view of the social world? What challenges did Emilie face? How did she overcome them? Does Emilie appear to be evidencing black feminist perspectives and stances? Why or why not?

In order to encourage students to take ownership of the discussion, organize the room in a Socratic seminar format to encourage deep thought and reflection on how Emilie viewed her world based on evidence from the assigned diary entries.[102] Depending on class size more time may need to be allotted for this component of the lesson.

**Closure** (10 minutes)

Point out overall observations about student understanding and learning based on class discussion during the Socratic seminar process. Reiterate to students that although they are attempting to make meaning of black feminism through the reading of texts in concrete and explicit ways, black feminism is in fact a complex and contested system of thought. Therefore, they should resist the temptation to seek "right" answers and interpretations and instead be willing to explore and integrate their understandings across multiple perspectives.

**Evaluation** (15 minutes)

Have students read Emilie's diary entries from January 1864 and complete an exit slip answering the following question: Is Emilie evidencing a black feminist perspective in this entry?[103] Why or why not? Encourage students to use class discussion and readings to support their answers. Based on student responses, consider how you may need to adjust or revisit key ideas in the next lesson.

**Homework**

Tell students to read Emilie's diary entries from 1864 (chapter 4) and look for evidence and contradictions related to Emilie's black feminist perspective.[104]

# DAY FOUR: *Reading black feminism in video clips and music lyrics*

**Warm-Up** (10 minutes)

Ask students to take out their comparative organizer and notes on the 1864 diary entries, and discuss evidence and contradictions related to black feminism.

**Group Exploration** (60 minutes)

Explain to students that today they will explore black feminist perspectives addressing educational and societal issues by reading video clips of speeches, documentary excerpts, and music with a black feminist lens.

Tell students they will read a series of media segments in their groups. Below is a list of possible video clips, lyrics, and magazine excerpts that can be explored by students. As students view each segment (and in some cases they'll need to view abbreviated segments) have them consider the following questions and track their responses:

- Who is the speaker/artist/writer?
- What can you tell about their background?
- What key ideas is the clip communicating?
- What is the purpose of the clip?
- How does the segment address black girls and women?
- What strategies for addressing concerns of black women and girls are being communicated in the segment?
- How does the clip confirm, problematize, or contradict ideas associated with black feminism?

*Video, music, and magazine excerpts*[105]

- Khadijah's Journey to Harvard: http://www.oprah.com/world/Khadijahs-Journey-to-Harvard-University-Video
- Chimamanda Ngozi Adichie TED talk—We Should All Be

Feminist: http://www.youtube.com/watch?v=hg3umXU_qWc
- Janelle Monae's "Ghetto Woman": http://www.youtube.com/watch?v=JugqJnLulmw ; *"Q.U.E.E.N."*: *http://www.youtube.com/watch?v=8ZXWzZ-GTgA*; *"Sincerely Jane"*: http://www.youtube.com/watch?v=M-kkaNYppcA
- Black Feminism Goes Viral by Jamilah Lemieux: http://www.ebony.com/news-views/black-feminism-goes-viral-045#ax-zz32CPgyxvt
- Michelle Obama "Weekly Address—Marks Mother's Day and Speaks Out on the Tragic Kidnapping in Nigeria: http://www.youtube.com/watch?v=PAncJ3nuczI
- Rock A Gele for Girls: http://www.youtube.com/watch?v=i8vwbT3Ndm8

**Closure** (10 minutes)

Bring students together and facilitate a discussion associated with their interpretation of black feminist perspectives in the clips

**Evaluation** (5 minutes)

Have students complete the exit slip below. Based on student responses, consider how you may need to adjust or revisit key ideas in the next lesson.

**Reading clips with a black feminist lens**

Create a chart that asks the following:
- Title of most impactful clip
- List two ways the clip is connected to key ideas related to black feminism.
- Would you recommend that your peers view this clip? Why or why not?

**Homework**

Tell students to read Emilie's diary entries from 1865.[106]
Ask students to search the web for a video resource that addresses

black feminism. Tell them to think about the types of video clips and lyrics explored in the class. Ask students to complete a final entry on the comparative organizer note-taking template based on the resource identified.

# DAY FIVE: *Black Feminist Performance Task*

**Lesson preparation:**

The last leg of the lesson plan set allows students to respond to a group performance task scenario that requires that they synthesize key ideas about black feminism and present their understandings to a school board. Since the task allows students to develop their presentation using various resources, mediums, and props (e.g., computer and internet, video recording devices, art, and costume), it is important to plan in advance to ensure students have appropriate resources to complete the task.

**Warm-Up** (10 minutes)

Ask students to take out their comparative organizer and meet in groups to discuss how the idea of black feminism was addressed in the video resource they found and consider similarities and differences between prior readings.

**Task preparation** (80 minutes)

Share the following task scenario with students: The local school board is reviewing a proposal to incorporate the study of black feminism in the high school curriculum. Before they make their final decision the school board is interested in hearing student presentations on the topic. Your group is charged with the task of convincing the school board that black feminism is a worthwhile and valuable area of study for high school students. Each group will have 15 minutes to present your position on black feminism to the school board. You can use music, video, Power-Point, prezi, lecture, visual art, performance, etc. to support your claims regarding black feminism. However, your presentation must clearly address the following questions:

What is black feminism? How can a black feminist lens allow you to critically read texts and the social world?

How does *Notes* address ideas related to black feminism? Why is

*Notes* an important text for students to read?

Why might some people view black feminism as an insignificant area of study? How would you respond to these claims?

Allow students to spend the remainder of class time developing the group presentation. Encourage students to refer back to graphic organizers, readings, videos, and music lyrics explored over the past few days in order to develop their presentations

**Homework**

If possible, tell students to meet with their group to revise, edit, and complete presentation ideas for the next class.

# DAY SIX: *School Board Presentation on Black Feminism*

**Lesson preparation:**

If possible, arrange to have adults or other teachers sit in as the mock school board and listen to the presentations. As the school board is listening to the presentations consider questions you may ask students to push their thinking and challenge the claims they make about black feminism.

**Presentations** (90 minutes)

Allow each group to present their presentations to the school board. After the presentations (if time permits) conduct a wrap-up class discussion on the most interesting, challenging, and useful ideas they learned during their study of black feminism.

# APPENDIX

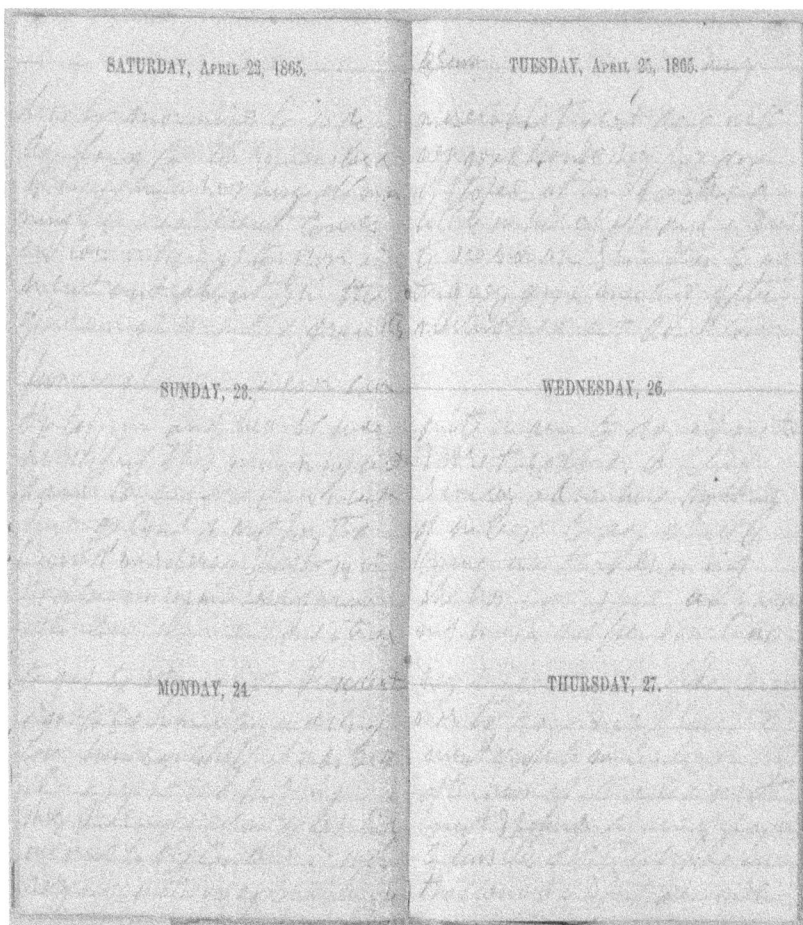

**Transcriptions**

*Friday, April 14, 1865*

To day is the day we celebrate the Soldier's Parrade. A flag was presented to the Regiment by the Bannekers. Very plesenit. Everybody seemed to have a holiday.

*Saturday, April 15, 1865*

Very sad news was received this morning of the murder of the President. The city is in deep morning. We were at meeting of the assossination (association). It decided to posphone the Fare (Fair).

*Sunday, April 16, 1865*

Very fine day. Everyone seems to partake of the solemnity of the times. Doct Jones spoke for us.

*Monday, April 17, 1865*

To day was set apart for a general holiday but seems to be a day of mourning. I went to Mr. Livelys then to school. Working was not very likely.

*Tuesday, April 18, 1865*

Nothing special on hand to day. I had meeting at eight. Very good meeting. After meeting Nellie and (I) went to Sarah Shims. Vincent invisible.

*Wednesday, April 19, 1865*

To day is a general holiday. The churches are open and the day has every appearance of Sunday. The President is concidered buried to day. I was out in the afternoon. We did not have church, Mr. Gibbs being away. Vincent was up a little while, as usal.

*Thursday, April 20, 1865*

Everything has a solemn afect. The streets look mournful. The people are sad. I went to Mr. Livelys in the afternoon. I did not get far for from it. Rained all the afternoon and evening. I spent the evening withe Nellie.

*Friday, April 21, 1865*

Cloudy and very dork (dark) morning. The funeral procession pass through tomorrow. I have not bin out to day. I am tired of the st(reet). Vincent was up this evening, He is so full of business.

*Saturday, April 22, 1865*

Lovely morning. To(day) is the day long to be remembered. I have bin very busy all morning. The President comes in town this afternoon. I went out about 3 in the afternoon. It was the grandest funeral I ever saw. The coffin and hearse was beautiful.

*Sunday, April 23, 1865*

This morning (I) went down to see the President but could not for the crowd. Mr. Robinson spoke for us in the afternoon, Very interesting sermon, after church, Vincent and I tried to get to see the President. I got to see him after waiting four hours and a half. It was actually a sight worth seeing.

**Pocket Diary** (students should be given copies so that they can make their own books)

*Date:* _____

_____

_____

_____

_____

_____

_____

_____

_____

# A Gateway to Freedom: Using the Diary Entries of Emilie Frances Davis To Study Philadelphia's Free Black Community

**Karsonya Wise Whitehead**

**Intended Audience:**

Secondary and Postsecondary Students

**Overview:**

In this lesson students will use a variety of primary and secondary sources including diary entries, maps, and editorials to learn explore some of the national events that were happening from 1863-1865. By the end of the lesson, students will be familiar with these events, the life of Emilie Frances Davis, and the impact of these events on Philadelphia's free black community. This lesson is intended for students who have already learned about American enslavement, the development of the free black communities, and the Civil War. Students should have some experience with conducting online research.

**Scope and Sequence:**

This lesson plan is designed to be used in conjunction with *Notes from a Colored Girl* and the digitized unedited diary entries located on Penn State's University Libraries website.[94] Although there are edited versions of the diary available in print and online, students are strongly encouraged to attempt to edit the diary entries for themselves before accessing the online versions.[95] Additionally, since the structure and order of this lesson plan can be varied, instructors should make adjustments to adapt the lesson plan to fit within their respective environments and with their students. This is a four-day lesson plan (depending upon your students) and students will need to have access to the Internet, both in school and at home. If they do not have access to the Internet, color copies of the

Davis diaries should be provided to them.

**National Standards for History**

Standard 3: Historical Analysis and Interpretation

- A. Compare and contrast differing sets of ideas, values, personalities, behaviors, and institutions by identifying likenesses and differences.
- B. Consider multiple perspectives of various peoples in the past by demonstrating their differing motives, beliefs, interests, hopes and fears.
- H. Hold interpretations of history as tentative, subject to changes as new information is uncovered, new voices heard, and new interpretations broached.
- J. Hypothesize the influence of the past, including both the limitations and opportunities made possible by past decisions.

**Common Core Literacy Standards in History/Social Studies**

- CCSS.ELA-Literacy.RH.11-12.1. Cite specific textual evidence to support analysis of primary and secondary sources, connecting insights gained from specific details to an understanding of the text as a whole.
- CCSS.ELA-Literacy.RH.11-12.2. Determine the central ideas or information of a primary or secondary source; provide an accurate summary that makes clear the relationships among the key details and ideas.
- CCSS.ELA-Literacy.RH.11-12.3. Evaluate various explanations for actions or events and determine which explanation best accords with textual evidence, acknowledging where the text leaves matters uncertain.
- CCSS.ELA-Literacy.RH.11-12.7. Integrate and evaluate multiple sources of information presented in diverse formats and media (e.g., visually, quantitatively, as well as in words) in order to address a question or solve a problem.
- CCSS.ELA-Literacy.RH.11-12.8. Evaluate an author's premises,

claims, and evidence by corroborating or challenging them with other information.

- CCSS.ELA-Literacy.RH.11-12.9. Integrate information from diverse sources, both primary and secondary, into a coherent understanding of an idea or event, noting discrepancies among sources.

## Objectives

- Interpret and evaluate primary and secondary sources and use them as tools to reconstruct history.
- Discuss the life, times, and experiences of Emilie Frances Davis and the nineteenth-century free black community.
- Articulate the impact of world events on Philadelphia's free black community in the struggle to build a viable and sustainable community and to end American enslavement.
- Debate and identify the strengths and weaknesses of their goals through comparative analysis.
- Evaluate the merits of these goals while placing them in a broader historical context.
- Identify and discuss two historical events that might have had a significant impact on the community.

## Essential Questions

- How can the diaries of Emilie Frances Davis be used to reconstruct history?
- How do the transcriptions of primary sources influence or change the interpretation of historical events?
- How did historical events around the country impact the lives and experiences of the free black community (through the eyes of one of its residents)?

# DAY ONE: She Who Believes in Freedom

**Motivation** (20 minutes)

Have the students either listen to or watch Sweet Honey in the Rock's *Ella's Song (We Who Believe in the Freedom Shall Not Rest)*.[96]

Have them write about what they think it meant to be "free" during the latter half of the nineteenth-century (1850-1865). If necessary, explain to them that approximately 90% of the black people in America where enslaved and were primarily situated in the southern half of the United States and that there was a large vibrant free black community primarily located in the North.

*Suggestion: In order to fully participate in and benefit from this lesson, students must understand the differences between the free and the enslaved communities. Take the time to explain this and to help them to understand that the history of black people in this country started with being indentured and then working towards freedom and not with being enslaved and then later freed. Students should also be made aware of the free black communities in Virginia and in Louisiana (time permitting, a discussion of the Louisiana Creole communities would be an interesting topic to explore).*

Invite students to share-out their responses to the prompt, taking time if needed to ensure that the students are clear on the differences between being freed and freeborn and between being mulatto and black. Explain to them that in 1860, these terms either allowed or prevented access to certain communities, churches, benevolent societies, and schools.[97]

**Small Group** (45 minutes)

Inform the students that they are going to spend the next four days discussing Philadelphia's free black community through the eyes and experiences of Emilie Frances Davis, a freeborn 19-year old mulatto woman who recorded her life and experiences in three years worth of pocket diaries.

Break them into small groups and provide them with a copy of the note-taking device.

Have them use the Internet to create a chart that highlights some of the key events that took place between 1863-1865, including the release of the Emancipation Proclamation, the assassination of President Abraham Lincoln, the ratification of the Thirteenth Amendment, and, the ending of the Civil War, to name just a few. These events should be listed in Sections I and II on the chart. *Depending upon your students, this may take two days to complete.*

## Note-Taking Device

| I. Date of the Event | II. Name and short description of the Event | III. Emilie's Diary Entry 1. Does she mention the event? 2. If not, what did she talk about? |
|---|---|---|
| January 1, 1863 | The release of Abraham Lincoln's Emancipation Proclamation, which freed all enslaved people living in states that were in rebellion against the Union (there were some exceptions to this). | Emilie wrote in her January 1, 1863 – that it was a "grand Jubilee" and that all of the churches were open. |

## Closure (10 minutes)

Bring the class back together and have them share-out all of the events. Create a list on the board and ask everyone to make sure that they have all of the same events (if key events are missing, take time to explain them and add them to the list).

## Homework

Have them read Chapter 2 from *Notes from a Colored Girl* to get an idea of what Emilie's life was like during that time. Tell them to take notes and to write down any words that are not familiar.

# DAY TWO: Primary vs. Secondary Sources

**Motivation** (10 minutes)

Ask the students to take out their homework notes to help create a biography about Emilie Davis.

Explain to them the differences between primary and secondary sources and tell them today they are going to use a primary source, Davis's diary, to complete Section III of their note-taking chart.[98]

**Small Group** (30 minutes, 15 minutes per group)

Put the students in small groups (different groups from yesterday) and assign them a year from Emilie Davis's dairy. Tell them to go through the diary and add all of the events onto their chart. Once finished, have students work in groups of three (one from the 1863, the 1864, and the 1865 group) to share their information.

**Whole Group** (10 minutes)

Lead the students in a short debriefing exercise, asking them to think about the following: *Is Emilie a reliable source that can be used to study events from 1863-1865? If not, explain why historians value primary sources over secondary sources (Emilie's diaries vs. a magazine article)? If so, explain why historians need to check other sources to correct and corroborate the diary entries?*

**Homework**

Have students log onto the University of Pennsylvania website and look at any page from the Emilie Davis diaries to see if they can transcribe it. Tell them not to use the book to check their transcriptions; instead, bring their assignment to class (in whatever state they are in) to discuss them.[99]

# DAY THREE: Reconstructing History

**Motivation** (10 minutes)

Tell students to work with a partner to check their transcriptions against Whitehead's transcription to determine how close they came to her transcriptions. Tell them that Whitehead's transcriptions are not the only version and that different scholars have looked at the diary entries and have come to different conclusion.

*Time permitting: students can go online and look at other transcriptions of the Davis diary.*

**Guided Practice** (15 minutes)

Provide students with a hard copy of Emilie Davis's 1865 "Abraham Lincoln" diary transcriptions and then project it on the screen and talk through the transcription process. Explain to them why the transcription process determines how the source is interpreted and then take a moment to talk about the importance of making methodological decisions. Have them look at Whitehead's "Editorial Methods" and then work together to agree on five methodological decisions that the class will use when they transcribe the Lincoln entries.

Working together as a group, transcribe the entries.

Ask them to think about the transcription process and reflect on the challenges and the rewards and why Editorial Methods are important.

**Final Project** (60 minutes)

*This project should be started in class and then completed at home.*

Students will create one-week's worth of diary entries from Emilie Davis's (fictional) 1866 pocket diary. They should look at the year and pick an interesting historical event and then record what they think that Emilie would have written about it. Once finished, they should be posted around the room for discussion. (A sample pocket diary page is included.)

# The Free Black Community and The Civil War

## Beau Lindesmith and Kelly D. Selby

**Intended Audience:**

Middle School Students

**Overview:**

This lesson focuses on free black community and the effect that the Civil War and the Emancipation Proclamation had on them. It uses the pocket diaries of a young black woman living in Philadelphia, Emilie Frances Davis, along with supporting secondary sources. Using multiple diary entries, written between 1863 and 1865, this lesson will highlight the experiences of her everyday life along with several historical moments. These entries give a voice to free black women who lived during the Civil War era. Combined with the secondary sources, these documents help students to understand a more complex story of this period in American history.

**Scope and Sequence:**

This lesson will take place during the Civil War and Reconstruction unit. In order to stimulate student thinking about life during the Civil War and to determine students' prior knowledge, the teacher will begin with a brainstorming session. The discussion should focus on what everyday life was like for free African Americans living in the northern states during the Civil War. The teacher will encourage students to raise their hands and share their ideas with the class. The teacher will take notes on the Smart Board, writing down key points. The teacher will then direct students to consider similarities and differences in the everyday lives of African American men and women. This activity will help students to understand that although much of the history of this period focuses on men, the experiences and contributions of black women is also important to understand.

Next, place students in small groups and give each group two sets of journal entries and a secondary source. Students will have a copy of both the translation and the actual journal entries written by Emilie Davis. They will read and annotate these, and will read secondary sources that explain significant events that occurred during the Civil War era. Each student group will read and discuss different everyday life experiences and historical events that occurred when Emilie Davis kept her pocket diaries, including church, celebrating special events, family, entertainment, the Emancipation Proclamation, and listening to Frederick Douglass. This will help students to understand the similarities and differences of the daily life of people who lived over one hundred and fifty years ago. Students will also learn how free African American women lived during this time. Students' understanding of the differences between primary and secondary sources will be reinforced. Students will show the ability to understand the entries through annotations, posters, and presentations.

After reading the primary and secondary sources, students will begin to apply what they have learned from the readings by creating group posters and oral presentations. Students should use pictures and text (including key ideas and vocabulary) on their group poster boards to describe their interpretations of the sources. This activity will be especially useful in those middle schools that have either reduced or cut Art classes from the curriculum. This will also provide the teachers with multiple opportunities to bring Language Arts into the classroom. Students will use their comprehension skills to explain what they have read and discussed about life for northern blacks during the Civil War. They will demonstrate this by creating a group poster and presentation. Each group will present their findings to the entire class, instead of using a general testing format, thus providing information on multiple subjects to each other. Students will complete their reading, discussion, and poster in three periods and will then present their interpretations to the entire class on the fourth day. The group presentations are another method to integrate Language Arts into the Social Studies classroom.

**National Standards for History**

*Historical Thinking Standards*

Standard 3B: Historical Analysis and Interpretation

- Consider multiple perspectives of various peoples in the past by demonstrating their differing motives, beliefs, interests, hopes, and fears.
- Compare and contrast differing sets of ideas, values, personalities, behaviors, and institutions by identifying likenesses and differences.

Standard 4: Historical Research Capabilities

- Support interpretations with historical evidence in order to construct closely reasoned arguments rather than facile opinions.

*U.S. History Content Standards for Grades 5-12*

U.S. Era 5: Civil War and Reconstruction (1850-1877)

Standard 2: The course and character of the Civil War and its effects on the American people

- A: The student understands how the resources of the Union and Confederacy affected the course of the war.
- B: The student understands the social experience of the war on the battlefield and home front.

**Common Core Standards Literacy in History/Social Studies**

- CCS.ELA-Literacy.RH.6-8.1. Cite specific textual evidence to support analysis of primary and secondary sources.
- CCS.ELA-Literacy.RH.6-8.2. Determine the central ideas or information of a primary or secondary source; provide an accurate summary of the source distinct from prior knowledge or opinions.
- CCS.ELA-Literacy.SL.6.5. Include multimedia components (e.g., graphics, images, music, sound) and visual displays in presentations to clarify information.
- CCS.ELA-Literacy.SL.7.5. Include multimedia components and visual displays in presentations to clarify claims and findings and

emphasize salient points.

- CCS.ELA-Literacy.SL.8.5. Integrate multimedia and visual displays into presentations to clarify information, strengthen claims and evidence, and add interest.

## Objectives
- Annotate, analyze, and evaluate primary and secondary sources on the daily life of northern blacks during the Civil War.
- Review and synthesize the everyday life activities along with significant historical events during the Civil War.
- Create group posters using drawings and text that demonstrate the students' interpretations of the sources. Present their finding in an oral presentation to the entire class.

## Essential Questions
- How did the Civil War effect free blacks in the north?
- What role did northern free black communities play in the destruction of slavery?

## Resources from *Notes from a Colored Girl*[107]
- Set A: January 1-3, 1863, November 18-20, 1863 (with annotation), and November 8-10, 1864
- Set B: June 18-20, 1863, June 30-July 2, 1863, February 9-11, 1864, and April 12-15 (with annotation)
- Set C: February 6-14, 1863, March 27 -30, 1864 (with annotation), and December 23-28, 1864
- Set D: March 17-19, 1863, April 25-27, 1863, and February 15-17, 1865
- Set E: April 13-24, 1865 and December 12-14, 1865
- Set F: The Emancipation Proclamation, 1863, Document Info, "100 Milestone Documents," Document Info, National Records and Archives Administration)[108]
- Set G: "Blue, Gray, and Black: African Americans in the Civil War," Pennsylvania Civil War 150[109]

- Set H: "People: Frederick Douglass," Frederick Douglass National Historic Site, National Park Service[110]
- Set I: The 13th Amendment, Document Info, "100 Milestone Documents," National Records and Archives Administration[111]

# DAY ONE: *The Civil War and Reconstruction*

**Class Discussion** (10 minutes)

Tell students to think about what the average person's life was like during the Civil War.

Write key ideas on the Smart Board for students to see. If necessary, take a moment to remind students about the Civil War and about the challenges faced by those at war and on the home front.

Explain to students that they will be researching various perspectives on the Civil War and will develop a poster project at the end of the lesson series.

**Small Groups** (30 minutes)

Divide students into small groups that contain five to six people.

Using the Primary Source package, pass out copies to each group (each group should receive a different set).

Explain to the students that they will have time to read the primary and secondary sources and will have time to discuss the key events and main purpose of the readings among their group. Students can create a table that helps them organize their ideas: a. Source (primary or secondary); b. Main purpose/Significance; c. Notes (comments or inferences drawn)

**Wrap-Up** (15 minutes)

Ask each group to share key events, purposes, and/or daily life observations of African American women based on their primary and secondary sources set.

# DAY TWO: *Interpreting Primary Sources*

**Small Groups** (20 minutes)

Provide each student with the transcribed copies of the primary sources for their group. Ask students to reread and complete text annotations in small groups.

**Class Discussion** (20 minutes)

Students will share their annotations and speak about the differences between primary and secondary sources in their groups. The teacher will move between groups to provide clarification and additional information.

**Group Project Overview** (10 minutes)

Create and pass out a grading rubric for the poster presentation and discuss the project.[112]

Explain to students that they will also be evaluated based upon the following questions:

- Do students understand the role of black northerners during the Civil War era?
- Can students explain what they learned from the sources by drawing and writing on the poster board?
- Do students fully understand the information that they read through the sources and understand life during this time for free northern blacks?
- Do students understand the difference between primary and secondary sources?
- Can students read and do their work on their own with time management skills?

The students should meet to plan out their poster drawings based on their interpretations of the documents. They should make a list of needed materials and should be encouraged to use the Internet to find and print pictures.

# DAY THREE: *Reflecting and Presenting History*

**Poster Development** (30 minutes)

Students will create drawings and provide text that explains their key interpretations on their poster board. The poster boards should include examples of the everyday life of black women, the key historical events presenting in the primary and secondary sources, and how the Civil War affected the northern black community.

Tell students that this project will be shared with the school's community and for some, this may be the first time that they learn about free black women during the Civil War, so their posters should include both a short historical write-up and clear pictures.

**Poster Presentation** (30 minutes)

Once the students have completed their poster boards (with drawings, key ideas, and vocabulary), they will set up their posters throughout the classroom. Students will participate in a gallery work, moving from poster to poster, and having the group provide a short presentation about their work. Students should be encouraged to take notes and ask questions. Time permitting, parents and/or other classrooms may be invited.

Once everyone has finished, students should take 5-minutes to reflect on what they learned about the free black community and free black women from this exercise. As students are sharing out, write down all of the key points on the Smart Board to ensure that everyone has received the same information.

# FUNctioning a Dress in Style

### Labonnie J. Wise

**Intended Audience:**
Middle School

**Overview:**

In this lesson, students apply their knowledge of unit rates to solve real-life math problems. Students will have an opportunity to explore how measurement conversions and proportional reasoning were used to design and create dresses during the late 1800s. Excerpts taken from the book, *Notes from a Colored Girl: The Civil War Pocket Diaries of Emilie Frances Davis,* are used as lenses for students to understand how measurement conversions and proportioning reasoning were influential in dress designing over 150 years ago.

**Common Core State Standards Connections**

- 5.MD.A.1. Convert among different-sized standard measurement units within a given measurement system (e.g., convert 5 cm to 0.05 m), and use these conversions in solving multi-step, real world problems.
- 6.EE.C.9. Use variables to represent two quantities in a real-world problem that change in relationship to one another; write an equation to express one quantity, thought of as the dependent variable, in terms of the other quantity, thought of as the independent variable.
- Analyze the relationship between the dependent and independent variables using graphs and tables, and relate these to the equation.
- 7.RP.A.2b. Identify the constant of proportionality (unit rate) in tables, graphs, equations, diagrams, and verbal description of

163

proportional relationships.

- 7.RP.A.2c. Represent proportional relationships by equations.
- 8.F.A.1. Understand that a function is a rule that assigns to each input exactly one output. The graph of a function is the set of ordered pairs consisting of an input and the corresponding output.

### Standards for Mathematical Practices

- MP1. Make sense of problems and persevere in solving them.
- MP2. Reason abstractly and quantitatively
- MP3. Construct viable arguments and critique the reasoning of others
- MP4. Model with mathematics
- MP5. Use appropriate tools strategically
- MP6. Attend to precision

### Objectives

- Examine the life of a black woman as a seamstress during the late 1800s.
- Explore examples of how measurements are used in our everyday lives.
- Discuss methods for solving problems involving unit rates.
- Discuss and compare solutions to measurement conversions and unit rate problems.
- Develop a rule that describes the relationship between the amount of fabric used and the amount of money earned.

### Essential Questions

- What is the role of measurements in clothing design?
- How is a ratio and unit rate used to compare two quantities?
- How does what I measure influence how we measure?
- What is a ratio as a measure of an attribute in a real world situation?

**Terms Used**

Have students work in teams to create a Frayer's Model chart (which includes a space for definitions, facts/characteristics, examples, and non-examples) so that they can define each of the following terms by grade level:[113]

- 6th grade: unit rate, ratio, proportion, and expression
- 7th grade: equation, expression, independent variable, and dependent variable
- 8th grade: equation, expression, inequality, independent variable, and dependent variable, function

Have them place their Frayer's Model charts on the wall so that students can refer back to it during the lesson.

# DAY ONE: *Measuring Up with Fabric*

**Motivation** (15 minutes)

Tell students that today they are going to look at the life of Emilie Frances Davis, a freeborn black woman, who lived and worked as a seamstress during the late 1800s. Have them study the *carte de visite* from *Notes from a Colored Girl* and compile a list detailing how this nineteenth-century dress is different from or similar to dresses that are currently worn.[114]

Have students work in pairs to think about how clothes were designed and created during the 1800s, specifically thinking about fabric, patterns, adornments, and length of dresses. Next, have students share their thoughts with the whole group.

**Class Practice** (20 minutes)

Tell the students that they are going to read excerpts from Emilie's life (see below) and that during the reading they should think about and make notes about some of the advantages that currently exist in the clothing industry that did not exist 150 years ago.

Have students keep a vocabulary log as they read through the excerpts, making notes of new words.

**Excerpts from** *Notes from a Colored Girl*

*The process of making a dress involved an extensive amount of time cutting the material. Dressmakers usually began by measuring and cutting out the pattern on muslin before cutting into the dress fabric. Muslin was a heavy cotton fabric that was sold plain and unbleached. For patterns it was cut to fit the body of the client, marked up with chalk or stitches, and held together by straight pins.*

*Cutting out the body of the dress was extremely laborious, took*

166

*almost as long as the sewing, and would typically be an all-day process.*

*The cutting and fitting had to be completed before corsets or stays were designed. The top portions of nineteenth-century dresses were usually cut very close to the body, and the bottom portions were wide and layered. Since women wore pannier hoop skirts under their dresses to extend the width of the dress, the fabric had to be cut wide enough to comfortably accommodate for it.*

*The cutting was completed in stages: the front was cut out first, then the sides, the centers, the collars, the material under the arms, the peplum (a short overshirt that is usually attached to a fitted jacket, blouse, or dress), and finally the linings. It took about twelve to fifteen yards of fabric to make a dress, and in addition to the cost of the fabric, dressmakers would charge approximately $50 (which is equivalent to $925) to complete the process.*[115]

Once finished, have them work independently to answer the following:

- What knowledge of measurements do you think Emilie had during the 1800s? *(The ability to understand feet and inches and the relationship between the two of them.)*
- How do you think she was able to design clothing by looking at a person? What mathematics skills was she using? *(By using estimation.)*
- Compare muslin material to calico material: what was the difference in cost (in the late 1800s) compared to difference in cost of its equivalency (today)? Write your answer as a ratio.
- Name the stages that Emilie used in order to design a dress.

Have them share out their answers and any words from their vocabulary list with the entire group.

Time permitting, give students a handout of the two different types of systems of units (English and SI). Discuss the difference between the English System of Metric Units and the International System of Units and explain the differences between the two.[116]

**Small Group** (10-12 minutes)

Have students work in pairs to list and share at least five units of measurements that they use every day.

Discuss unit conversions. Give examples of how students convert from inches to yards to feet. Have them work in pairs to complete the tables below.

| Units of Measurements (in yards) | Convert to inches | Convert to feet |
|---|---|---|
| 12 | | |
| 13 | | |
| 14 | | |
| 15 | | |

Have students share their solutions with the entire group, generating a discussion around conversions to include possible incorrect solutions.

**Wrap Up** (10-12 minutes)

Have students complete the math task, "Converting Fractions of a Unit Into a Smaller Unit," taken from Illustrative Mathematics for further practice.[117] Exit Slip: Give students an index card and tell them to jot down one thing that they learned today (keep these as they will be used at the end of each of the lessons).

# DAY TWO: The Cost of Fitting to Size

**Motivation** (10-15 minutes)

Give students an index card and tell them to write down two ways that unit rates are used in their everyday lives. Have students stand up and share their answers and then call on another student to share out what they wrote. Have students cross out their responses if someone else has mentioned it. Continue until all responses have been shared. Take a minute or two to clear up any misconceptions.

**Class Discussion** (10 minutes)

Discuss how to find the unit rate using ratios. Give students a few examples of unit rate problems.

Revisit the discussion on converting units of measurements and tell them that they are going to use what Emilie earned for each dress to calculate the amount of money she may have earned based upon the amount of fabric that used in yards, inches and feet.

**Small Group** (20 minutes)

Have students work in small groups of three or four to complete the problem below: *If Emilie charged $50 dollars to design and create dresses, how much did her clients pay per unit of fabric for each designated amount of fabric?*

| Amount of fabric used (in yards) | Unit rate (dollars/yard) | Unit rate (dollars/feet) | Unit rate (dollars/inches) |
|---|---|---|---|
| 12 | | | |
| 13 | | | |
| 14 | | | |
| 15 | | | |

Have students compare their solutions and share their responses with the group. Where (unit rate) did Emilie earn the most amount of money?

Where (unit rate) did she earn the least of money? What accounts for the differences in calculations?

**Wrap-Up** (10 minutes)

Have students complete the math task, "Mangos for Sale," taken from Illustrative Mathematics for further practice.[118] Exit Slip: Give students back their index cards from yesterday and have them add another line stating the most important things that they learned today.

# DAY THREE: *Woman Versus Machine*

**Motivation** (15-20 minutes)

Have students read the excerpts from *Notes from a Colored Girl* (see below) focusing on the following questions:

- What happened to Emilie in 1865?
- Name two advantages and two disadvantages of Emilie using a sewing machine compared to sewing dresses by hand.
- How much time did it take Emilie to design and make Mary's wedding dress if she began at 6 a.m., assuming she worked until the next morning?
- What did Emilie do as a career outside of making dresses and which job potentially earned her the most money?
- Have students keep a vocabulary log as they read through the excerpts, making notes of new words.

**Excerpts from *Notes from a Colored Girl***

*In 1864, Emilie, along with many women around the country, purchased her first sewing machine. She either paid for the entire amount up front or she participated in Singer's hire purchase or installment plan, with five dollars down (equivalent to $92.50) and regular monthly payments. Singer's rigid- arm sewing machine with an overhanging arm, a table, and a foot treadle sold for approximately $75 (equivalent to $1,387.50).*

*One year later, in 1865, Emilie was hired to design and make the* crème de la crème *of a dressmaking enterprise: "Very busy, making Mary's wedding dress. Sewing untill after 1'o clock." Since wedding dresses were made using the finest fabric and were usually very elaborate and detailed, dressmakers would normally charge two to three times their going rate. Emilie probably* *charged anywhere from $55 to $150 (equivalent to $1,017.50 to $2,775).*

*Although she did not mention it throughout the month, the fact that she was able to complete the dress while still managing her domestic work would have been very difficult if she did not have a sewing machine at her disposal.*[119]

Once finished, have students share out both their responses and any words from their vocabulary list with the entire group.

**Small Group** (20 minutes)

Have students work in small groups to solve the math task, "Chocolate Bar Sales," taken from Illustrative Mathematics and then have them share out their answers with the whole group.[120]

**Wrap Up** (10 minutes)

Give students back their index cards and tell them to look at what they have already learned and then add the most important thing that they have learned today. Have students share-out this information.

# DAY FOUR: Pulling It All Together

**Small Grouping** (30 Minutes)

Have students work in small groups of two or three to answer the following: *Using the yards of fabric in the table, determine the amount of money Emilie earned designing wedding dresses, assuming constant proportionality.*

| Amount of fabric used (in yards) | Amount of money earned (in dollars) |
|---|---|
| 12 | $150.00 |
| 13 | $162.50 |
| 14 | |
| 15 | |
| F | |

- Identify the independent and dependent variables.
- Write an equation that expresses the amount of fabric in terms of cost.
- How much would it cost to make a dress with 20 yards of fabric?
- *(For advanced students: Write a compound inequality that represents the amount of fabric used. Write a compound inequality that represents the amount of money earned.)*

**Wrap-Up** (15 minutes)

Have students reflect on the ways in which Emilie's life improved once she purchased a sewing machine and then have them briefly think about whether or not Emilie would have been as successful as a seamstress today as she seems to have been from 1863-1865.

# The Ordinary Made Extraordinary: Understanding Diary-Writing and Living Through History with Emilie Davis

## Rebecca D. Hunt & Joseph E. Flynn, Jr.

**Intended Audience:**

High school students

**Overview:**

This lesson explores the importance of diary writing and the importance of appreciating one's day-to-day activities as being a part of a larger, national history. Using the pocket diaries of Emilie Davis, students will analyze and critique the life of Emilie as represented in her diaries. Students will also consider how Emilie's diary is a precursor to contemporary forms of diary writing (i.e. blogs, Tweets, Facebook, etc.). Overall, students will have the opportunity to consider the importance of their own unique experiences and how they are always located in significant historic events.

**Scope and Sequence:**

First, students will be introduced to journaling as an important and useful tool for documenting and understanding history. Second, students will begin with a broad conceptualization of both the Civil War and the state of free African Americans in the 1860s through documentaries and short readings. This lesson is designed assuming a block schedule in which a class period is approximately 80 minutes. Revise as necessary.

### Common Core Standards for Literacy in History/Social Studies

- CCS.ELA-Literacy.RH.9-10.1. Cite specific textual evidence to support analysis of primary and secondary sources, attending to such features as the date and origin of the information.

- CCS.ELA-Literacy.RH.9-10.3. Analyze in detail a series of events described in a text; determine whether earlier events caused later ones or simply preceded them.
- CCS.ELA-Literacy.RH.9-10.4. Determine the meaning of words and phrases as they are used in a text, including vocabulary describing political, social, or economic aspects of history/social science.
- CCS.ELA-Literacy.RH.9-10.7. Integrate quantitative or technical analysis (e.g., charts, research data) with qualitative analysis in print or digital text.
- CCS.ELA-Literacy.RH.9-10.9. Compare and contrast treatments of the same topic in several primary and secondary sources.
- CCS.ELA-Literacy.RH.9-10.10. By the end of grade 10, read and comprehend history/social studies texts in the grades 9-10 text complexity band independently and proficiently.
- CCS.ELA-Literacy.RH.11-12. Cite specific textual evidence to support analysis of primary and secondary sources, connecting insights gained from specific details to an understanding of the text as a whole.
- CCS.ELA-Literacy.RH.11-12. Determine the central ideas or information of a primary or secondary source; provide an accurate summary that makes clear the relationships among the key details and ideas.
- CCS.ELA-Literacy.RH.11-12.5. Analyze in detail how a complex primary source is structured, including how key sentences, paragraphs, and larger portions of the text contribute to the whole.
- CCS.ELA-Literacy.RH.11-12.9. Integrate information from diverse sources, both primary and secondary, into a coherent understanding of an idea or event, noting discrepancies among sources.
- CCS.ELA-Literacy.RH.11-12.10. By the end of grade 12, read and comprehend history/social studies texts in the grades 11-

CCR text complexity band independently and proficiently.

## National Standards for History
*Chronological Thinking*
- Distinguish between past, present, and future time.
- Identify the temporal structure of a historical narrative or story: its beginning, middle, and end (the latter defined as the outcome of a particular beginning).
- Establish temporal order in constructing their [students'] own historical narratives: working forward from some beginning through its development, to some end or outcome; working backward from some issue, problem, or event to explain its origins and its development over time.
- Interpret data presented in time lines and create time lines by designating appropriate equidistant intervals of time and recording events according to the temporal order in which they occurred.
- Reconstruct patterns of historical succession and duration in which historical developments have unfolded, and apply them to explain historical continuity and change.

*Historical Comprehension*
- Identify the author or source of the historical document or narrative.
- Appreciate historical perspectives—the ability (a) describing the past on its own terms, through the eyes and experiences of those who were there, as revealed through their literature, diaries, letters, debates, arts, artifacts, and the like; (b) considering the historical context in which the event unfolded--the values, outlook, options, and contingencies of that time and place; and (c) avoiding "present-mindedness," judging the past solely in terms of present-day norms and values.

*Historical Research Capabilities*
- Formulate historical questions from encounters with historical documents, eyewitness accounts, letters, diaries, artifacts, photos, historical sites, art, architecture, and other records from the past.
- Obtain historical data from a variety of sources, including: library and museum collections, historic sites, historical photos, journals, diaries, eyewitness accounts, newspapers, and the like; documentary films, oral testimony from living witnesses, censuses, tax records, city directories, statistical compilations, and economic indicators.
- Support interpretations with historical evidence in order to construct closely reasoned arguments rather than facile opinions.

## Objectives
- Identify significant events that occurred during the last years of the Civil War, 1863-1865.
- Compare and contrast the daily life of Emilie Davis with popular assumptions about African American life during the Civil War.
- Categorize and analyze the roles free African Americans played during the Civil War.
- Explain and critique the roles of African American women during the Civil War.
- Explain and generalize the possible effects the Civil War had on free African Americans.
- Determine the differences between diary writing and journaling.
- Differentiate and compare/contrast tools that can be used for diary writing, historically and contemporarily.
- Create a diary of one's own life during a set period.
- Evaluate a tool for use in personal diary writing.

**Essential Questions**

- How is journaling about one's day-to-day experiences an important part of documenting history?
- What are the popular beliefs about the lives of African Americans during the Civil War compared to what is represented in the pocket diaries of Emilie Davis?

**Instructional Note**

This lesson can be constructed to utilize the entire diary of Emilie Davis or excerpts from the diary. Special considerations should be made for length of class periods, recurrence of class periods, reading levels of students, time in the semester/school year, and other factors unique to each teacher.

# DAY ONE: *An Introduction to African Americans, the Civil War, and Diaries*

**Motivation** (15 minutes)

Tell the students that they will be spending the next few days learning about the day-to-day life of an African American woman during the Civil War and that for the next two weeks they will have the opportunity to engage in diary writing about their own lives.

Explain that the use of diaries has been and continues to be a valuable source for understanding history across time periods and locations.

Ask the students to activate prior knowledge by asking them what they know about the Civil War. Next, ask them to think more deeply and brainstorm what they know about the lives of African Americans during the Civil War. Once their ideas have been exhausted and listed, ask them what they think they would like to know about people's daily-lived experiences during the Civil War. Be sure to save the comments students offered, as they will need to be reminded of them later.

Finally, have the students consider all of the fundamentals of a diary.

**Shared Reading**

(20-25 minutes)

Point out to the students that there are differences between diaries and journals.

Divide the students into small groups of 3-5 each. Ask the students to do a shared reading of at least one short article about the differences between diary writing and journals.[121]

**Class Discussion**

(10-15 minutes)

After students have read and discussed the article(s) in their small groups, facilitate a large-group discussion about the similarities and differences of diaries and journals, tying what they learned from the reading and discussion to what they brainstormed earlier.

After the large-group discussion, ask the students to summarize what they have learned and offer your own summary to reiterate the key points.

## Evaluate (5 minutes)

To assess student learning, share with them two one-page handouts (one of a diary and one of a journal) and ask them to label each as either a diary or journal. This should be done individually rather than as a group.

Introduce Emilie Davis and her diary (use the introduction of this text for background information). Then, give the students a collection of excerpts that you find most compelling or interesting for them to read and annotate. The students will have to read the number of pages you choose (this choice should be made in consideration of students' ability levels, time available, and depth of exploration).

# DAY TWO: *Further Considering the Lives of African Americans During the Civil War*

**Warm-Up** (10-15 minutes)

Ask students to share what they remember from the previous class. If they are struggling or have questions, review the previous class's key ideas. Share with the students their comments/brainstorming about the lives of African Americans during the Civil War from the previous day.

**Documentary Screening** (60 minutes)

Let the students know that today's class will focus on the lives of African Americans before and during the Civil War and that they will be watching a documentary about African Americans during the Civil War.[122] (Documentaries can be long, typically an hour runtime. Teachers will have to be cognizant of their time constraints and may have to select relevant portions/scenes rather than screening the entire documentary.) As guiding questions for the day, consider the following (questions can be projected onto a Smart Board or given as a handout):

- How are the lives of African Americans characterized through the documentary?
- What were some of the struggles African Americans had to face?
- Who were some of the key or important people mentioned in the documentary and why were they important?
- Did the documentary provide a view into the daily lives of African Americans? If so how? If not, why?
- What were the key or interesting ideas for you as you watched the documentary?
- Additional questions that can either be asked prior to or after the movie:
- What did you know about African Americans and the Civil War before the documentary?

- What new information did you learn about African Americans and the Civil War by watching the documentary?
- How has your thinking about or understanding for African American life during the Civil War changed?

**Post Screening Discussion** (20 minutes)

After screening give the students 4-5 minutes to free-write their thoughts/reflections about the film.

Then, ask the students to join in small groups to revisit the questions and their answers. Give students an opportunity to change or add to the answers (depending upon your class, students can use a graphic organizer, like a KWL chart, to guide them during the discussion).

After the small group discussion reconvene the large group and take 5-10 minutes to share reflections.

**Touching Base Discussion** (15 minutes)

Although this class session may have a great deal of information and discussion it is fundamentally important to reconnect the students back to Emilie's diary. Engage in an open discussion about the diary and the excerpts selected for reading. Keep the discussion limited to the knowledge and comprehension levels of Bloom's Taxonomy.[123] The discussion is simply to ensure that students are reading the diary and to assess how comfortable they are with the book and the diary entries. Try to make sure there is at least 10-15 minutes for this final discussion. Possible questions include:

- What are some of the day-to-day activities that Emilie chronicled in her diary?
- How can you tell that the diary was written during the Civil War?
- Who were some of Emilie's friends?
- How is the diary different from other forms of writing, such as a short story or a newspaper or magazine article?

**Evaluation** (5 minutes)

Before ending class, as a form of assessment, ask students to write down three new ideas they learned about African American life during the Civil War through the documentary and/or Emilie's diary.

**Homework**

Finally, for at home reading, assign more excerpts. The amount of reading should be indicative of reading comprehension levels and other relevant factors. As stated before, teachers can assign the entire reading before the unit begins, or one year for each day of class, or a series of selected excerpts.

# DAY THREE: *Understanding Emilie and the Exceptionality of the Mundane*

**Warm-Up** (15 minutes)

Ask the students to reiterate key and/or interesting ideas from the previous class. After a short discussion of the previous class, ask the students the following question: What makes a life extraordinary? Allow the students a moment to consider the question before discussing. Then ask the students if Emilie was extraordinary during her time?

Share with the students the idea that all humans are extraordinary, in part because we all typically live through extraordinary times and do small things daily that show perseverance, ingenuity, amity, care, and community. Emilie is an interesting person because: 1) as pointed out in the introduction of this text, hers is one of the only diaries from an African American woman during this time period that remains; 2) Across her entries she is a woman committed to her work, her friends, her family, and her community; 3) She is a free woman living during a time when freedom was in a precarious state for people who looked like her; 4) She showed a great deal of commitment by chronicling her daily life for three years (teachers should feel free to embellish this list; these are only suggestions to frame the day).

**Partnerships** (10 minutes)

For the first activity, ask students to work in pairs. Each pair will create a schedule of the day based on Emilie's diary. To frame the activity ask the students: What is a typical day for Emilie? After the pairs create a day, ask the students to compare/contrast Emilie's typical day with their own. This can be done in their pair or can be a whole group discussion after a few groups have shared their day schedules.

**Small groups** (15-20 minutes)

Next, split the students into three groups and assign each group a year from Emilie's diary. If the groups are more than five students in each group, the teacher can decide to double the number of groups to six and assign a year to two groups that work independently of one another. In the event that teachers are only having students read excerpts rather than the whole diary be mindful of selecting excerpts that represent each year.

## Comparative Timeline (30 minutes)

Inform the students that they will be creating a comparative timeline that chronicles both the events of Emilie's life as represented in her diary and major events of the Civil War. The teacher can allow students to use either their textbooks or a website and encourage them to use more than one timeline from the Internet as a way of increasing their knowledge of important Civil War events.[124]

Using butcher paper and markers give the students time to create a timeline for the year the group was assigned. Across the top of the timeline identify key events of the Civil War and across the bottom of the timeline identify key events in the life of Emilie. This part of the class should take approximately 30 minutes.

## Whole Class Share (15 minutes)

Give the students an opportunity to share their timelines.

## Wrap-Up (10-15 minutes)

Ask students to share their perceptions of Emilie's day and events of the Civil War. Then, ask them what major events they are living through right now (or since they were born). Ask them to consider and discuss how national and world events have an impact on their daily lives. Be sure to highlight the fact that even as major, nation-changing events happen, life still goes on and the mundane tasks of everyday continue. Finally, ask them what makes each of them extraordinary and, then reiterating a question from earlier ask, is Emilie an extraordinary person? (These are, of course, rhetorical questions but they are the kinds of questions that can be used to spur further discussion.)

# DAY FOUR: *Applying What We Know about Emilie to Our Daily Lives*

**Warm-Up (15 minutes)**

Ask students to reiterate key and/or interesting ideas from the previous class. After a short discussion of the previous class, ask the students the following question: What is the difference between journals and diaries? Allow students a moment to consider the question before discussing.

Share examples of journals and diaries with the students. The examples can be visual images of journals and diaries or have actual journals and diaries for the students to examine. It is important that students understand the difference. Explain to the students why Emilie used a diary. It is known that paper and writing instruments were not readily available to everyone. The fact she had access to the diary and the writing instruments was very fortunate for a free woman living during a time that people who looked like her were not free to read and write.

**Small groups (15 minutes)**

Ask students which types of social media are available today to document daily activities and depending upon your access to technology, have students log on and read through a Twitter feed. Ask them to think about some of the limitations with using social media to document your life. Time permitting, students can also scroll through Facebook (sharing their own pages, if they are appropriate) or at online blogs.[125]

**Social Media Assignment (10-15 minutes)**

Next, have students select one media tool they are willing to use to chronicle their lives. The selection can come from the list they helped to create or they have the opportunity to select some other medium.

After each student has selected their social media tool, explain that they will keep a "diary" of their daily activities for two weeks. Provide the students with the actual beginning and ending dates. Keep a record of the social media tools for each student. Be prepared to have a few students requesting to use an actual diary.

Provide instructions on how the diaries will be submitted and assessed, tailored to each teacher's unique contexts and resources.

If time permits, have each share which media tool they will be using with an explanation of why.

## Wrap Up (10 minutes)

Explain to the students the importance of writing in their diaries every day. Emphasize how Emile took time each day to write in her diary and the commitment she made by chronicling her daily life for three years during one of the most important and violent eras in the history of the United States. Furthermore, reiterate that even though her daily entries may be read as mundane, uneventful, or even pointless (for some) Emilie, through her process of daily repetition, actually shows the beauty, power, and extraordinary of the day-to-day.

## Project Wrap Up (In two weeks, 15 minutes)

Over the next two weeks, remind students of their diary writing assignment, checking in with them and encouraging them to continue with the project. Three days before the final assignment is due, select one or two students to share the entry that they wrote on the first day of the assignment (this is to encourage the students to keep up with the project).

On the day that the assignment is due, collect all of the journals and give them to another student to see if they can go through them and create a timeline of events. Time permitting, students can reflect on the project and/or share out some of their diary entries.

# Exploring the Democratic Narratives of Free Black Women

## Kent A. McConnell

**Intended Audience:**

High School and College Students

**Overview:**

The cultural and scientific methodological assumptions that once girded a single narrative or simple retelling of the nation's past have been under siege for decades. Among the numerous arguments that critics offer as evidence is the loss of historical objectivity and the rise of relativistic historical analysis. This argument, however, is predicated on cultural assumptions and philosophical biases that all-too-readily exclude women, minorities, and the working class from full participation in the nation's current public life or give credit to their contributions to our historical past. The lesson plan that follows attempts to provide students with a theoretical framework in which to negotiate United States history and deconstruct the work and writings of nineteenth-century free black women.

### Scope and Sequence

Through the frequent and repeated use of popular primary resources these lessons encourage students to familiarize themselves with the nation's ever-expanding print resources. Their task is two-fold: first, to uncover evidence that will help them to understand the varied lives of free blacks and slaves during the Civil War Era and second, to begin to contextualize elements of everyday life in the industrializing northeast seeing the way large historical processes had both beneficial and negative consequences in the lives of ordinary citizens. By reading excerpts from the work of W.E.B. Du Bois, students examine how a noted African

American contemporary of Emilie Frances Davis thought about the problem of race and class in America. Through the use of critical thinking skills and creative exploration of primary sources, students develop a greater sense of historical thinking while being asked to compare a variety of topics to the realities of an "ordinary" life of an African American female revealed in Davis's diary. Through this evaluative process, students begin to appreciate how the sub structural realities of the nation's growing industrial and urban order profoundly shaped the lives of free blacks who lived in the North during the Civil War Era. Finally, instructors should see the series of exercises below as a process acquiring disparate elements of historical knowledge that should be winnowed into interpretive themes and a final project such as a research paper, presentation, documentary film, or other significant measure for the course. The sample series of lesson plans below utilize a research paper as its method of evaluation.

## National Standards for History
*Standard 1: Chronological Thinking*
- Identify the temporal structure of a historical narrative or story
- Establish temporal order in constructing historical narratives of their own.
- Reconstruct patterns of historical succession and duration; explain historical continuity and change.
- Compare alternative models for periodization.

*Standard 3: Historical Analysis and Interpretation*
- Compare and contrast differing sets of ideas, values, personalities, behaviors, and institutions by identifying likenesses and differences.
- Consider multiple perspectives of various peoples in the past by demonstrating their differing motives, beliefs, interests, hopes and fears.
- Hold interpretations of history as tentative, subject to changes as new information is uncovered, new voices heard, and new inter-

pretations broached.

- Hypothesize the influence of the past, including both the limitations and opportunities made possible by past decisions.

*Standard 4: Historical Research Capabilities*
- Formulate historical questions
- Obtain Historical data from a variety of sources.
- Identify the gaps in the available records, marshal contextual knowledge and perspective of the time and place.
- Support interpretations with historical evidence

*Standard 5: Historical Issues—Analysis and Decision-Making*
- Identify issues and problems in the past.
- Marshal evidence of antecedent circumstances.
- Identify relevant historical antecedents.
- Evaluate alternative courses of action.

## Objectives

- Annotate, analyze, and evaluate the central arguments outlined in primary as well as secondary materials.
- Review, relate and synthesize elements of primary documents to broader historical processes.
- Write a critical analytical essay taking a position one on the many themes developed in these lessons such as: gender, class, race, religion, or the American Civil War.

## Essential Questions

- How does the record of Emilie Frances Davis's life challenge or shape our presumptions about the past, particularly when it comes to understanding the lives of African American women and men?
- To what degree did new industrial opportunities shape the lives of everyday people in the North? Do you think these forces positive ones in the short and long run?

- How is Davis's life a reflection of the "negotiated boundaries" of freed blacks in the North during the Civil War era? What challenges are apparent for Davis in her everyday life and how did she use these to her benefit?
- To what degree do you think race and class shape the lives of the majority of Americans in the mid-nineteenth-century?

# DAY ONE: The Emancipation Proclamation: Race and Receptivity

**Preparatory Work:**

In preparation for the day's discussion on race and public reaction to the Emancipation Proclamation, several perspectives are warranted in order to facilitate nuanced interpretations among students. Instructors may wish to assign other readings or spread these preliminary readings over two days.

**Independent work** (10 minutes)

First, begin by having students read the Emancipation Proclamation taking notes on Lincoln's executive order. Encourage students to frame questions about the text during their annotation process. This exercise should be completed before any other reading is done.[126]

Next, students should have some grounding in secondary analysis of the Emancipation Proclamation and its immediate and long-term significance.[127]

Assign students brief selections of primary text reading from Emilie Frances Davis diary concerning the American Civil War.

*Extension activity: depending upon your students, have them search for and read one or two newspaper articles related to the issuance of the Emancipation Proclamation. Direct their research to articles that appeared in the winter and early spring of 1863.*[128]

**Broad Classroom Discussion** (20 minutes)

Depending upon your classroom either show the students a short online video featuring a panel discussion on Lincoln or have them reflect on the different ways that the Emancipation Proclamation may have been received (for example, how would the free black community have interpreted this document differently from the white communities in the North).[129]

As a large group, lead students through a discussion of the Proclamation highlighting the student's annotation of the text.

**Small Group Shared Reading and Exploration** (20 minutes)

Next break students into small groups assigning one or two of the following short letters or publication to each group. Ask students to measure the commentary in these primary documents against their newspaper article/newspaper research. Some nineteenth-century contemporary sources for consideration are:
- Letter from Frederick Douglass to Major George L. Stearns, August 1863
- Letter from Abraham Lincoln General Nathaniel P. Banks (Louisiana) on Reconstruction, August 5, 1863
- Letter from Abraham Lincoln to James C. Conkling on Emancipation, August 26, 1863
- Horace Greeley, "A Prayer for Twenty Millions," New York Tribune, August 20, 1862[130]

**Class Discussion** (15 minutes)

Given the varieties of interpretations and reaction to Lincoln's Emancipation Proclamation, explore with students ideas about how nineteenth-century Americans understood the document in comparison to how we see it today.

**Closure** (10 minutes)

After completing the close reading and discussion ask students to revisit the central themes of the broader group discussion and then revisit the key points they noted in their separate commentary. Tell them to think through their original answers and see if there is anything that they would change or add.

**Evaluation** (10 minutes)

To close the session and assess student learning, have them write a short reflection on what the Emancipation Proclamation meant to

Lincoln's contemporaries in achieving social equality and civil justice. Ask them to speculate on why Emilie Frances Davis chose to begin her diary on the day the document was released. Was the starting point of Davis's autobiographical effort simply coincidental to this date or was something else motivating her?

## Homework

Split the students into two groups. Give one group a reading on African American economic and social life and the other group a reading on nineteenth-century African American life in Harrisburg, PA (Given that Davis visited and had friends in the Harrisburg area).[131]

## DAY TWO: Emilie Frances Davis and Domestic Production in the Civil War Era

**Class Discussion** (15-20 minutes)

Introduce the class to the expansion of economic activity and the transformation of everyday life by comparing the 1840s to the 1870s (possible lecture points could include the advent of important technological developments, the advent of commercial photography, the rise of the newspaper culture, the introduction of the sewing machine, the telegraph, or the transportation revolution).

Ask students to comment on why they feel these developments were important. Help them to identify the importance of changes in both sub structural realities and super structural ideals.[132]

**Small Group Shared Reading and Exploration** (20 minutes)

Break the classroom into small groups making sure male and female voices are represented in each group.

Ask the students to identify passages in Emilie Frances Davis that illustrate the industrial and technological changes that were reshaping everyday life and providing both opportunities and limitations to Emilie's life.[133]

**Closure** (15 minutes)

Close the discussion by asking students to offer an overarching evaluation of the changes experienced by black Pennsylvanians during this era. Do they feel Emilie understood these forces of change as a positive thing and how do they measure the significance of these changes in the direction of Emilie's life?

**Homework**

Have students read a selection from Catherine Clinton's *The Other Civil War: American Women in the Nineteenth Century*.[134] Tell them to pay particular attention to what the author writes about free black women in the North during the Civil War Era.

Ask students to annotate their work, calling attention to ideas they find interesting or to areas of the text they feel need further clarification.

Remind students that they should be thinking about their research paper topics and creating thematic hubs of inter-related information for later interpretation.

*Extension Activities: Briefly introduce the life of W.E.B. Du Bois to students discussing his significance to the debate on class and race in the late nineteenth-century and beyond. Pre-select intellectually provocative excerpts from W.E.B. Du Bois's* Black Reconstruction in America 1860–1880 *that highlight a central theme and may help to develop an argument for their papers. Read the passage and briefly discuss pointing out the presuppositions of the writer and guiding points of his argument.*[135]

## DAY THREE: Exploring Gender, Race, and Class in the North

**Open Classroom Discussion** (15-20 minutes)

Gather students in a group to either read aloud their textual annotations or summarize their interests in areas of the text. Summarize the students' ideas categorizing information where possible. Make sure information/summary is available to them during small group work time.

**Individual Research/Exploration** (25 minutes)

The intention of this exercise is to allow students time to build upon the previous days discussion and to begin developing a richer appreciation of how communities of women were formed and many times thrived in light of the marketplace forces afoot in America. In order for this exercise to work, students should have access to computers with Internet capability or copies of the material should be made available to them.

Read the following line to students: "...the very act of reading novels and newspapers established a new kind of mental community based on a version of Newtonian time. I also reinforced...expectations that human actions in society, like motion in nature, could be explained in terms of scientific cause and effect" and have them reflect on what this means.[136]

Direct students to use the resources from the week thus far to illustrate ways this statement is true.[137]

Ask students to take meticulous notes on what they find. Make sure they record important language and events that appear in these articles in addition to the resource title and dates.

**Homework**

Have students think and write about the importance of religion and the church in the life of Emilie Frances Davis.[138]

# DAY FOUR: *The Ties That Bind:*
## *Religious Life and Social Organizations at the Midcentury*

**Background Discussion** (25 minutes)

Briefly introduce the importance of religion among nineteenth-century African Americans.[139]

Conduct a group-shared reading and ask the students to identify passages in Emilie Davis's work that talk about her views on religion. Pay particular attention to the nuances of Davis's religious life that happens both within traditional religious circles, but elsewhere including her attention to church members and the death of friends.

Close the discussion by asking students to offer an overarching evaluation of the meaning of Emilie's religious expression. Can we see how religion was liberating to freed blacks like Emilie?

**Further Exploration—Small groups** (20 minutes)

Break the classroom into small groups making sure male and female voices are represented in each group.

Ask the students to consider other elements of religious life or other social organizations that were important in shaping Davis's independent spirit.

Gather students around hubs of computers for further exploration of this topic focusing on nearby African American communities in Pennsylvania using the following newspapers: Philadelphia's The Evening Telegraph and Lancaster's Daily Intelligencer.[140]

Close the discussion by asking students to offer an overarching evaluation of the changes experienced by black Pennsylvanians during this era concerning their religious lives or social networks. Do they see African Americans gaining greater strengths and enjoyments through the development of these networks? How do these networks offer support, entertainment, or create opportunities for African Americans? What resistance do they encounter at the time?

## Homework

Assign students an excerpt from W.E.B. Du Bois's *Black Reconstruction in America*.[141] Ask them to annotate their work paying particular attention to the themes and underlying assumptions of the writer's argument.

## DAY FIVE: *Writing Her Way Into History*

**Evaluation** (60 minutes)

On Demand Critical Essay: Tell students that they are going to write a critical essay taking a position on some element of the life or of a theme that appears in the diary of Emilie Francis Davis. The students should cite the scholarship used during the week, using evidence from primary and secondary resources to support their position. If taking on larger arguments about the historical legacy of economics and race in America, students should also reference current examples to support their claims.

**Closure** (20 minutes)

Once the students have completed their essays, revisit the essential questions of these lessons asking students to relate their papers and findings to the discussion. What was of interest to them when doing their research? How did an examination of primary materials shape their thinking about class and race in America?

**Independent Research Activities**

Students can explore the University of Virginia's online electronic database, "The Valley of the Shadow Project."[142] Of particular interest are the "Letters & Diaries" section of the website, as well as "Census & Tax Records" of the antebellum period. Students can also explore what it meant to be an ordinary women by researching Harvard University Library's Open Collections Program "Women Working, 1800 – 1930."[143] Of particular notice are the "Books and Pamphlets," "Diaries and Memoirs," "Institutional Records," and "Manuscripts" links.

# CONTRIBUTORS

**Calvin Coleman is** a self-taught artist who incorporates abstract expressionism and Fauvism; Coleman builds upon the canvas with an assemblage of heavy body acrylic paint, a variety of textiles and other mediums to embellish his uninhibited style of painting. After graduating from Lincoln University, where he earned his B.S. degree in Early Childhood Education, Coleman taught at the elementary level for fourteen years. Works by Calvin Coleman are included in numerous public, private collections and publications including the Embassy of Rome, Italy, and the permanent collection of the City of Atlanta Housing and Urban Development; Lincoln University, PA; and Drexel University.

**Conra D. Gist, Ph.D.,** is assistant professor of curriculum and instruction at the University of Arkansas. She received her Ph.D. from the City University of New York (CUNY). Her primary research interests focus on teacher diversity, culturally responsive pedagogy, and teacher learning.

**Megan Fisher** is a 2014 graduate of Loyola University Maryland.

**Joseph E. Flynn, Jr., Ph.D.,** is associate professor of curriculum and instruction at Northern Illinois University. He teaches courses related to social justice and multicultural education, curriculum studies, and the nature of educational change and reform. His scholarship offers critical examinations of Whiteness Studies, media and popular culture, and curriculum. Previously, he has guest edited a special edition of *The Black History Bulletin* on the role of African Americans in popular culture. Currently, he is co-editor of the Woodson Review and he is co-editing a book entitled *"A Rubric Nation: Critical Inquiries into the Impact of Rubrics on Education"* (2014).

Rebecca D. Hunt, Ph.D., is an assistant professor in the Department of Educational Technology, Research and Assessment at Northern Illinois University. She received her M.A. in Library and Information Science from the University of Alabama. Her research interests focus on culturally relevant pedagogy in Library Science, school library services for K-12 students, and diversity in literature for children and young adults. She currently serves as president-elect for the School Media Technology Division of the Association for Educational Communication and Technology (AECT); serves as chair for the American Library Association Stonewall Book Award Committee and a committee member of the American Association of School Libraries (AASL) Research and Statistics Committee.

Beau Lindesmith is a History and Integrated Social Studies double major at Walsh. He has served as a high school offensive line football coach for the past three years. He will student teach in Fall 2014, and graduate in December 2014. He co-wrote this lesson plan as a requirement for his Pre-Student Teaching Methods class.

Kent A. McConnell, Ph.D., is a member of the History Department at Phillips Exeter Academy in New Hampshire. Prior to Exeter, he served for four years as a visiting professor in the Department of History at Wake Forest University. His publications and areas of research interest include mid- to late-nineteenth-century America. He co-edited the publication, *Conflicts in American History: A Documentary Encyclopedia, The Gilded Age, Progressive Era, and World War I: 1877–1920* and is completing his monograph *A Time-Stained God: Religious Lives, Civil War Deaths and the Remaking of God in America* forthcoming with Cambridge University Press. Dr. McConnell has held several regional research fellowships and national fellowships, including ones with the National Endowment for the Humanities and the Pew Charitable Trust.

Alicia L. Moore, Ph.D., holds the Cargill Endowed Professorship in Education at Southwestern University, Georgetown, Texas. Specializing in multiculturalism and culturally responsive teaching (CRT), accommodations and modifications for diverse populations, and early childhood best practice, Dr. Moore's areas of research include the experiences of African American students at predominantly white institutions of higher education, the perceptions of white pre-service teachers regarding culturally responsive teaching and the culturally responsive teaching of young children. She is the co-editor of the Black History Bulletin (BHB).

**La Vonne I. Neal, Ph.D.,** is dean of the College of Education and a professor of special education at Northern Illinois University and facilitator for the Association for the Study of African American Life and History (ASALH) Teachers' Workshop. She is the co-editor of the Black History Bulletin (BHB) and the co-editor, along with Christine E. Sleeter and Kevin K. Kumashiro, of the forthcoming *Diversifying the Teacher Workforce: Preparing and Retaining Highly Effective Teachers* (Routledge, 2014).

**Kelly D. Selby, Ph.D.,** is associate professor of History in the Department of the Humanities and the   Secondary Education Social Studies Content Coordinator for the Division of Education at Walsh University, where she is also the Faculty Advisor of the Alpha Nu Sigma chapter of Phi Alpha Theta. She is a member of the Ohio Humanities Council Speaker's Bureau, the advisory committee for Ohio Civil War 150, and an executive board member on the Ohio Academy of History.

**Paula Stanton** is a proud graduate of Anacostia Senior High School, Howard University, and Southeastern University in Washington, DC. She is a veteran teacher with 20 years of classroom teaching experience. In addition to teaching middle and high school students, she has held several leadership positions, including high school English specialist, Site Director of non-profit teacher preparation program, and English department chairperson.  She is the acting English Department chairperson at a local Maryland high school and a master teacher for the Better Lesson NEA Master Teacher Project. She is currently pursuing a PhD in K-12 Leadership at Walden University. Her current research interest is retention of alternatively certified teachers in urban school districts.

**Noël Voltz** is currently a doctoral candidate in the field of African American History at the Ohio State University. More specifically, she is a scholar of early African American History particularly focusing on women of color in the United States and the Atlantic World. Her dissertation, titled, "'It's no disgrace to a colored girl to placer': Sexual Commodification and Negotiation Among Louisiana's 'Quadroons,' 1805-1860" seeks to understand how free women of color used sex across the color line as a tool of negotiation in various literal and figurative spaces in antebellum Louisiana. She will graduate with her Ph.D. in December 2014.

**Jeanine L. Williams, Ph.D.,** is assistant professor and Coordinator of Reading Acceleration Initiatives at The Community College of Baltimore County. Dr. Williams has ten years of experience teaching developmental reading. In addition, she has published and presented nationally on critical literacy and other non-traditional approaches to postsecondary literacy instruction. She holds a Ph.D. in Language, Literacy, and Culture from the University of Maryland, Baltimore County.

**Labonnie J. Wise, M.Ed.,** is the Lead Clinical Faculty in Mathematics at the Urban Teacher Center. She has extensive background in developing mathematics and science curriculum as well as training elementary, middle, and high school teachers. She earned her M.Ed. in Curriculum and Instruction/special Education and a B.S. in Chemical Engineering from Howard University.

**Karsonya Wise Whitehead, Ph.D., is** assistant professor of communication and African and African American studies in the Department of Communication at Loyola University Maryland; a Master Teacher in African American History for intermediate, secondary and college teachers; the 2007 Gilder Lehrman *Preserve America* Maryland History Teacher of the Year; and, a three-time New York Emmy-nominated documentary filmmaker. She has received various fellowships including the NEH Summer Stipend (2010) and the Gilder Lehrman Fellowship (2013). Dr. Whitehead is the author of *Notes from a Colored Girl: The Civil War Pocket Diaries of Emilie Frances Davis* (USC Press, 2014), *Sparking the Genius: The Carter G. Woodson Lecture* (Apprentice House, 2014), and the forthcoming *The Emancipation Proclamation: Race Relations on the Eve of Reconstruction* (Routledge, fall 2015). She received her Ph.D. in Language, Literacy, and Culture from the University of Maryland, Baltimore County.

# End Notes

1    Patricia Hill Collins, *Black Feminist Thought: Knowledge, Consciousness, and the Politics of Empowerment*, 2nd Ed. (New York: Routledge, 2000), 104.

2    Karsonya Wise Whitehead, *Notes from a Colored Girl: The Civil War Pocket Diaries of Emilie Frances Davis*. (South Carolina: University of South Carolina Press, 2014),14.

3    Collins, *Black Feminist* Thought, 2.

4    Whitehead, *Notes from a Colored Girl*, 4.

5    Walker, qtd in Collins, *Black Feminist Thought*, 2.

6    bell hooks, *Teaching to Transgress: Education as the Practice of Freedom*, (New York: Routledge, 1994), 14.

7    For more on the ways in which this absence impacts the classroom, see Jessica B. Schocker in "Representing African American Women in U.S. History Textbooks" in *The Social Studies, 104* (1), (2013), 23-31; Collins, *Black Feminist Thought*,1-8.

8    For more on how knowledge streams change over time, see and compare the early research on the life of Malcolm X to Manning Marable's *Malcolm X: A Life of Re-invention* (New York: Penguin Books, 2011) or the main steam work on Abraham Lincoln to Lerone Bennett, Jr.'s *Forced into Glory: Abraham Lincoln's White Dream* (Chicago: Johnson Publishing Company, Inc., 2000).

9    Whitehead, "They Both Got History: Using Diary Entries to Analyze the Written Language and Historical Significance of Free Black Philadelphia," *LLC Review* (2009), 48-61; Whitehead, *Notes from a Colored Girl*, 4.

10   Wise also offers a similar pathway in her science lesson plan, *It's Raining Again: Discovering Science in the Diaries of Emilie Frances Davis*, which explores weather patterns and meteorology. For more, see www.kayewisewhitehead.com (Accessed 24 May 2014).

11   *Whitehead's Note: In my book, *Notes from a Colored Girl*, I explained how my research with Emilie was multidisciplinary, where I used tools from the fields of journalism, history, historical sociolinguistics, and documents editing. During this process, of preparing this book for print, I realized that the term "multidisci-plinary" was not the correct term for what I was doing. I needed a bigger term, a more inclusive term. This is where the idea of viewing this work as a practice in *transdisciplinarity* began. I believe that this work on Emilie both *crosses* disciplines and *goes beyond* them; thus a lesson plan on Emilie's work as a seamstress can go beyond math to include history (by researching the role of black women as business women), English (by researching the language that Emilie uses to describe her work), social and cultural mores (Emilie's ability to move between two social circles, as both a domestic and a seamstress), marketing (Emilie's ability to copy dress patterns), fashion (Emilie's use of cotton versus muslin or calico fabric), slavery (by comparing Emilie's life as a seamstress to the life of Elizabeth Keckly, Mary Todd Lincoln's dressmaker) and so on. Whitehead, *Notes from a Colored Girl*, 4.

12   Geneva Gay, *Culturally responsive teaching: Theory, research, & practice*, (New York: Teachers College Press, 2010).

13     Whitehead, *Notes from a Colored Girl*, 61.

14     India Arie "Just Do You," (song lyrics). http://www.azlyrics.com/lyrics/indiaarie/justdoyou.html (Accessed 24 May 2014).

19     In her book, *Alice Walker and Zora Neale Hurston: The Common Bond*, Lillie P. Howard writes that Alice Walker was a responder to the call of Zora Neal Hurston thus making them sisters and heiresses to the African oral tradition. Mary Faggan Churchill's review of *Alice Walker and Zora Neale Hurston: The Common Bond* in Melus, Vol. 22, No. 3, Varieties of Ethnic Criticism (Autumn, 1997): 199-202. http://www.jstor.org/stable/467664 (Accessed 2 June 2014); Alice Walker, "Looking for Zora" on Teacher Web. http://teacherweb.com/CA/NewburyParkHighSchool/bond/LookingforZora-AWalker-3.pdf (Accessed 2 June 2014).

20     This term grew out of my weekly conversations with my mentor, Dr. Martha Wharton, who helped me to develop and define my process. For more on training students to become forensic herstorical investigators, see "They All Got History: Notes on Becoming a Forensic Herstorical Investigator."

21     In the 1860 U.S. Census, her Ladies Union Association's records, and on her death and marriage certificates, Emilie's name is spelled Emily. In the front of her diaries she wrote Emlie and Emilie. I selected Emilie as it seemed to be the spelling that she preferred and the spelling that she used for her daughter's name.

22     Emilie lived at 916 Rodman Street, between South and Lombard with Elijah J., Sarah, Elizabeth, and Thomas. Based on how she spoke about Elijah and his age, I suggest that he was probably her uncle and that Elizabeth and Thomas were her siblings.

23     On the 1860 U.S. Census, Emilie is listed as being 21 years old so at this time she would have been about 24.

24     Emilie wrote about attending classes during the evening and based upon some of the teachers that she mentions and some of her friends, I concluded that she attended ICY.

25     I later changed the term home sewer to the more sophisticated term of a seamstress since she seemed to be more experienced than a "home sewer."

26     According to the U.S. Census, Emilie's father was from Maryland (he was probably born enslaved as he is listed as Colored on the Census) and her mother was from Pennsylvania.

27     I have not been able to find any additional information about Emilie's mother or additional information about her sister. There is a possibility that her sister may have had a daughter.

28     There is no else in Emilie's who is written about as much as Nellie. She was mentioned 504 times and though I have not found any information about her (Emilie never mentions her last name), I do not believe that they were sisters. I believe that they were best friends and confidantes, and perhaps (though I do not know for sure), even more. To put this number in context, Emilie mentioned Vincent—her beau, the one who she claimed she "could not get along" without—213 times.

29     I have not been able to find any information about Edmond.

30     In addition to this entry, Emilie also racially self-identified in the Memoranda section of 1864 pocket diary where she writes, "On Saturday 25, I visited ther(re?) with Mrs. Wister. It certainly was worth going to. We visited all of the principle places of interest when I cam out. I had seen so much I hardly could recollect what I had seen. I saw a great deal of hansome work but I did not see any done by my *colored* people" (emphasis mine). (Whitehead, 2014, p. 144)

31    Since Emilie often mentioned Nellie and Cristy together and since she called her Mrs. Cristy at one point, I concluded that Cristy and Nellie were married. I have not been able to confirm this. It appears instead as if Nellie and Cristy were just dating as he is only mentioned in relation to Nellie from January 1863 – April 1864.

32    Although she never refers to her sister by name, Emilie does mention her often. She writes of sending and receiving letters and of having her come and visit in May 1865.

33    In her later entries, Emilie becomes more actively in the war efforts. She works with her club, the Ladies Union Association, to raise money for the black soldiers in South Carolina; she attends lectures where Frederick Douglass talks about the recruitment efforts; and, she sells tickets to concerts given by the Hutchinson Family Singers (an abolitionist singing group). Additionally, many of her friends and family members (including Elijah, Alfred, and Thomas) were either drafted or they enlisted in the armed services.

34    Perhaps not frivolousness but Emilie does spend more time writing about herself than about what was happening in the world around her.

35    In 1866, Emilie, for reasons unknown, married George Bustill White and she either chose to stop writing in a pocket diary or they have yet to be found. Her choice of a mate is really interesting because from 1863-1865, when she wrote over 30,000 words about her life, she never mentioned George by his full name. She wrote about five Georges and only two by their full name: George Freeman and George Fulner. Emilie and George had 5-6 children together. I have been able to find her marriage and death certificate and information about where she was (is) buried.

36    Although she frequently lamented about being alone, during a typical Emilie had frequent visitors and made several visits.

37    I have not been able to find her father's address in Harrisburg. I know that her dad was from Maryland and that he had been born enslaved but I am not sure how or when he made his way to Philadelphia.

38    This transcription was completed using my black and white copies; once, I was able to study Emilie's diary, using a magnifying glass and taking color pictures, the actual transcription reads, "Very cold. This day I have looked forward to withe dread. Poor Alfred we buried this afternoon. No one but him that knows all things knows my feelings. If it is the Master's will I hope I never will have another day like yesterday." (Whitehead, 2014, p. 212)

39    See earlier note about the Civil War and about how Emilie was aware of what was going on and she did write about it.

40    Emilie actually wrote this on the last page of the 1865 diary. It appears as if she later inserted the word "is" (since the original sentence is written in pen and the word "is" is in pencil).

41    She actually worked for four families.

42    REFERENCES: Blassingame, J. W. (1975). Using the Testimony of ex-slaves: Approaches and problems. *Journal of Southern History*, 41(4), 480-485; Bloom, L. Z. (1996). 'I write for myself and strangers': Private diaries as public documents. In S. L. Bunkers, & C. Huff (Eds.), *Inscribing the daily: Critical essays on women's diaries* (pp. 25-30). Amherst, MA: University of Massachusetts Press; Chisholm, D. (2005). *Queer constellations: Subcultural space in the wake of the city*. Minneapolis, MN: University of Minnesota Press; Diaries of Emilie Davis, 1863-1865. Unpub-

lished raw data. Archives of the Historical Society of Pennsylvania, Philadelphia, PA; Du Bois, W. E. B. (1996). *The Philadelphia Negro* (reprinted ed.). Philadelphia, PA: University of Pennsylvania Press; Fasold, R. (1981). Tense marking in Black English: A linguistic and social analysis. Washington, DC: Center for Applied Linguistics; Hershberg, T. (1981). Free Blacks in Antebellum Philadelphia: A study of ex-slaves, freeborn and socioeconomic decline. In T. Hershberg (Ed.), *Philadelphia: Work, space, family, and group experience in the nineteenth century, essays toward an interdisciplinary history of the city* (pp. 368-391). New York, NY: Oxford University Press; Hershberg, T. & Williams, H. (1981). Mulattoes and Blacks: Intra-group color differences and social stratification in nineteenth century Philadelphia. In T. Hershberg (Ed.), *Philadelphia: Work, space, family, and group experience in the nineteenth century, essays toward an interdisciplinary history of the city* (p. 392 - 434). New York, NY: Oxford University Press; Hine, D. C. (1994). *Hine sight: Black women and the re-construction of American history.* Brooklyn, NY: Carlson Publishing; Kautzsch, A. (2002). *The historical evolution of earlier African American English: An empirical comparison of early sources.* New York, NY: Mouton de Gruyter; Krapp, G. (1924). The English of the Negro. *American Mercury*, 2, 190-195; Kroch, A. (1995). Dialect and style in the speech of upper class Philadelphia. In G. Guy, J. Baugh, D. Schiffrin, & C. Feagin (Eds.), T*owards a social science of language: Papers in honor of William Labov* (Vol. 1, pp. 23-46). Philadelphia, PA: John Benjamins Publishing Company; Kurath, H. (1929). *Black English: Its history and usage in the United States.* New York, NY: Random House; Labov, W. (1972). *Language in the inner city: Studies in the Black English Vernacular.* Philadelphia, PA: University of Pennsylvania Press; Labov, W. (1994). *Principles of linguistic change: Internal factors.* Philadelphia, PA: Wiley-Blackwell; Labov, W. & Harris, W. A. (1986). De facto segregation of black and white vernaculars. In D. Sankoff (Ed.), *Diversity and diachrony* (pp. 1-24). Amsterdam, Netherlands: John Benjamins Publishing Company; Montgomery, M., Fuller, J. M., & DeMarse, S. (1993). "The black man has wives and sweet harts [and third person plural -s] jest like the white men": Evidence from verbal -s from written documents on 19th-century African American speech. *Language Variation and Change*, 5, 335–357; Perdue, C. Jr., Barden, T., & Phillips, R. K. (Eds.) (1992). *Weevils in the wheat: Interviews with Virginia ex-slaves.* Charlottesville, VA: University of Virginia Press; Poplack, S. (2000). *The English history of African American English.* Malden, MA: Blackwell Publishers Inc.; Rawick, G. A. (Ed.) (1977). *From sundown to sunup: The making of the black community* (Vol. 1). Santa Barbara, CA: Greenwood Press Paperback; Royster, J. J. (2000). *Traces of a stream: Literacy and social change among African American women.* Pittsburgh, PA: University of Pittsburgh Press; Salvatore, N. (1996). *We all got history: The memory books of Amos Webber.* New York, NY: Times Books; Smith-Rosenberg, C. (2004). The female world of love and ritual: Relations between women in nineteenth-century America. In L. K. Kerber & J. S. De Hart (Eds.), *Women's America: Refocusing the past* (pp. 168-182). New York, NY: Oxford University Press. Tapia, J. (1998). The schooling of Puerto Ricans: Philadelphia's most impoverished community. *American & Education Quarterly*, 29(3), 297-323; Welter, B. (1996). The cult of true womanhood. *American Quarterly.* 18(2), 151-174; Wolfram, W. (1969). *A sociolinguistic description of Detroit Negro speech.* Washington, DC: Center for Applied Linguistics; Wolfram, W. & Schilling-Estes, N. (2006). *American English: Dialects and variation* (2nd ed.). Malden, MA: Blackwell Publishing.

43 I made the decision to add punctuation and words that I thought were missing (based on context clues), and to silently correct spelling errors. My goal was to present a user-friendly text that people could read, understand, and (hopefully) enjoy.

44 "Emilie Davis" Philadelphia: The Great Experiment. https://www.youtube.com/watch?v=F-6jVnVQ1Kc (Accessed 2 June 2014); "Emilie Davis' Journal" Philadelphia: The Great Experiment. https://www.youtube.com/watch?v=ZE2txjLvbq4 (Accessed 2 June 2014).

45 "They Both Got History: Using Diary Entries to Analyze the Written Language and Historical Significance of Free Black Philadelphia." In LLC Review 2009: 48-61; "Reconstructing the Life of a Colored Woman: The Pocket Diaries of Emilie F. Davis." In The Pennsylvania Magazine of History and Biography, Vol. 135, No. 4 (October 2011): 561-564.

46 Karsonya Wise Whitehead, "With All Deliberate Speed," The National Visionary Leadership Project. http://www.visionaryproject.org/teacher/lesson2/wordsphrases.html (Accessed 27 May 2014).

47 These are merely suggestions and teachers should think about finding other blogs that may connect directly with your community (maybe a daily blog written by one of your teachers or a leader in your community.)

48 Whitehead, *Notes from a Colored Girl*, 185-187.

49 For more on Emilie's work as a seamstress, see *Notes from a Colored Girl*, 160-164.

50 If students do design a new cover, please feel free to share them with Dr. Whitehead at her website: www.kayewisewhitehead.com.

51 "Female Heroines of the Civil War," https://www.youtube.com/watch?v=f0RLo-jCEj7o (Accessed 24 May 2014).

52 Whitehead, *Notes from a Colored Girl*, 18-61.

53 For more on the history of journals, see Whitehead, *Notes from a Colored Girl*, 6, 146-148.

54 "Memories of Childhood's Slavery Days http://docsouth.unc.edu/fpn/burton/burton.html (Accessed 24 May 2014).

55 "Poll Everywhere" http://www.polleverywhere.com/k12-student-response-system (Accessed 24 May 2014).

56 "Emancipation Proclamation" http://www.archives.gov/exhibits/featured_documents/emancipation_proclamation/transcript.html (Accessed 24 May 2014).

57 "Digital History Frederick Douglass's Timeline" http://www.digitalhistory.uh.edu/exhibits/douglass_exhibit/douglass_timeline.html (Accessed 24 May 2014).

58 "Frederick Douglass's Top 10 Quotes" https://www.youtube.com/watch?v=Z5Ya-JH2BF24 (Accessed 24 May 2014).

59 Literacy stock photos and images. http://www.canstockphoto.com/images-photos/literacy.html

60 Whitehead, *Notes from a Colored Girl*, 76-79.

61 Whitehead, *Notes from a Colored Girl*, 64-65, 76-77, 80-81, 84.

62 "Frederick Douglass" http://en.wikipedia.org/wiki/Frederick_Douglass (Accessed 24 May 2014)

63 Whitehead, *Notes from a Colored Girl*, 39, 45, 57-58.

64 "Our Work is Not Done" http://teachingamericanhistory.org/library/document/our-work-is-not-done/ (Accessed 24 May 2014).

65 "Learning to Read and Write" http://www.pasadena.edu/files/syllabi/dlbronstein_29682.pdf (Accessed 24 May 2014).

66    "Malcolm X" http://en.wikipedia.org/wiki/Malcolm_X (Accessed 24 May 2014).

67    "Who Taught You to Hate Yourself." http://www.youtube.com/watch?v=gRS-gUTWffMQ

68    "Learning to Read" excerpt from *The Autobiography of Malcolm X*. http://www.smccd.net/accounts/bellr/readerlearningtoread.htm (Accessed 24 May 2014).

69    "President Barack Obama" http://www.whitehouse.gov/administration/president-obama (Accessed 24 May 2014).

70    "Barack Obama on Education" http://www.youtube.com/watch?v=DQ5kqTcXfTk (Accessed 24 May 2014).

71    "Remarks by the President on a World-Class Education" http://www.whitehouse.gov/the-press-office/2014/01/30/remarks-president-world-class-education (Accessed 24 May 2014).

72    Whitehead, *Notes from a Colored Girl*, 3-4.

73    In *Notes from a Colored Girl*, Whitehead writes that the story of Emilie Frances Davis begins on January 1, 1863 as "the nation has gone through a climatic socio-political shift in thinking and being." It was during this time, as the "albatross of slavery" was being removed that Davis sat down to write. Whitehead, 17.

74    Whitehead, *Notes from a Colored Girl*.

75    Images and text from the Emile Davis diary can be found in Whitehead's book and also online at the following website: http://davisdiaries.villanova.edu/january-7-9-1863/ (Accessed 24 May 2014).

76    Mary Lynn Rampolla, *A Pocket Guide to Writing History, Fifth Edition* (Boston: Bedford/St. Martin's, 2007), 6.

77    Examine "A World Discovered" to find additional supporting information. Whitehead, *Notes From a Colored Girl*, 1-17.

78    Whitehead, *Notes from a Colored Girl*, 8, 160-172.

79    For digital copies of the Philadelphia inquirer, visit the Olive Civil War archive. http://archive.olivesoftware.com/Default/Skins/CivilWarNB/Client.asp?Skin=CivilWarNB&GZ=T&AppName=2 (Accessed 24 May 2014).

80    For digital images and transcriptions of Emilie Davis's diaries, see Villanova University – Falvey Memorial Library. "Emilie - Memorable Days: The Emilie Davis Diaries," Villanova University. http://davisdiaries.villanova.edu/march_2-4_1863/ (Accessed 24 May 2014).

81    Use Whitehead's work to gather this information. Whitehead, *Notes from a Colored Girl*, 160-172.

82    For more information, see Lydia Lucas, "The Historian in the Archives: Limitations of Primary Source Materials," *Minnesota History* 47 (Summer 1981), 227-232.

83    Whitehead, *Notes from a Colored Girl*, 16.

84    Patricia Collins, *Intellectual activism*. (Philadelphia, PA: Temple University Press, 2012).

85    Collins, *Intellectual Activism*, 22.

86    Ibid, 18.

87    Patricia Hill Collins, *We Who Believe in Freedom Cannot Rest: Lessons from Black Feminisms*, http://www.youtube.com/watch?v=36Iq8XkfQ-0 (Accessed 24 May 2014).

88    Patricia Hill Collins, *Fighting Words: Black Women and the Search for Justice*. (Minneapolis, MN: University of Minnesota Press, 1998).

89    Alice Walker, *Anything We Love Can Be Saved: A Writer's Activism*, (New York:

Ballantine Books, 1997).

90    Collins, *Intellectual Activism*.

91    bell hooks, *Black looks: Race and representation*, (Boston, MA: South End Press,1992).

92    Common Core ELA and Literacy Standards in Social Studies, http://www.core-standards.org/ELA-Literacy/RH/11-12/ (Accessed 24 May 2014).

93    Patricia Hill Collins, *Intersecting Oppressions*: http://www.uk.sagepub.com/upm-data/13299_Chapter_16_Web_Byte_Patricia_Hill_Collins.pdf (Accessed 24 May 2014); bell hooks, *Black Women Shaping Feminist Theory*: http://projects.ecfs.org/fieldston57/us45/Readings/hooksFeminism.pdf (Accessed 24 May 2014); Additional book ideas and selected chapters can be found on the 'MHP' Black Feminism Syllabus: http://www.msnbc.com/melissa-harris-perry/the-mhp-black-feminism-syllabus (Accessed 24 May 2014); Other writers to consider include Patricia Williams, Alice Walker, Kimberlé Williams Crenshaw, Beverly Guy Sheftall, Ann duCille, and Hazel Carby, to name just a few.

94    "The Emilie Davis Diaries," http://www.libraries.psu.edu/psul/digital/davisdiaries.html (Accessed 7 February 2014).

95    Whitehead, *Notes from a Colored Girl*.

96    Sweet Honey in the Rock, "Ella's Song." http://www.youtube.com/watch?v=U6Uus--gFrc (Accessed 24 May 2014).

97    See Whitehead's "Editorial Methods" and "A World Imagined" for more information about the difference between the terms. *Notes from a Colored Girl*, xiii-xvii; 62-85.

98    "Primary and Secondary Sources." http://www.princeton.edu/~refdesk/primary2.html (Accessed 2 June 2014)

99    "The Emilie Davis Diaries," http://www.libraries.psu.edu/psul/digital/davisdiaries.html (Accessed 7 February 2014).

100   Whitehead, *Notes from a Colored Girl*, 4-5.

101   Ibid, 18-61.

102   Socratic Seminar: https://www.teachingchannel.org/videos/teaching-the-n-word (Accessed 24 May 2014).

103   Whitehead, *Notes from a Colored Girl*, 105-106.

104   Ibid, 105-145.

105   All websites accessed on 24 May 2014.

106   Whitehead, *Notes from a Colored Girl*, 173-213

107   Whitehead, *Notes from a Colored Girl*, 18-19, 23-24, 28, 31-33, 38-40, 56, 110, 115-117, 139, 143-144, 179, 211

108   "Emancipation Proclamation (1863)," 100 Milestone Documents, National Archives and Records Administration, accessed March 22, 2014, http://www.ourdocuments.gov/doc.php?flash=true&doc=34 (Accessed 24 May 2014).

109   "Blue, Gray, and Black: African Americans in the Civil War," Pennsylvania Civil War 150, accessed March 21, 2014, http://pacivilwar150.com/ThroughPeople/AfricanAmericans/HistoricalOverview (Accessed 24 May 2014).

110   "People: Frederick Douglass," Frederick Douglass National Historic Site, National Park Service, accessed May 21, 2014, http://www.nps.gov/frdo/historyculture/people.htm (Accessed 24 May 2014).

111   "13th Amendment to the U.S. Constitution: Abolition of Slavery (1865)," 100 Milestone Documents, National Archives and Records Administration, accessed March 22, 2014, http://www.ourdocuments.gov/doc.php?flash=true&doc=40

(Accessed 24 May 2014).

112    Sample poster presentation rubric: http://www.readwritethink.org/files/resources/lesson_images/lesson1076/rubric.pdf (Accessed 24 May 2014).

113    http://www.worksheetworks.com/miscellanea/graphic-organizers/frayer.html (Accessed 24 May 2014).

114    Whitehead, *Notes from a Colored Girl*, 162.

115    Whitehead, *Notes from a Colored Girl*, 160-164.

116    Metric Handout. http://web.ics.purdue.edu/~braile/eas100/metric.pdf (Accessed 22 May 2014); National Institute of Standards and Technology, "The International System of Units (SI)." http://physics.nist.gov/Pubs/SP330/sp330.pdf (Accessed 22 May 2014).

117    http://s3.amazonaws.com/illustrativemathematics/illustration_pdfs/000/000/293/original/illustrative_mathematics293.pdf?1390749147 (Accessed 24 May 2014).

118    Illustrative Mathematics, www.illustraivemathematics.org; http://s3.amazonaws.com/illustrativemathematics/illustration_pdfs/000/000/077/original/illustrative_mathematics_77.pdf?1390749348 (Accessed 24 May 2014).

119    Whitehead, *Notes from a Colored Girl*, 162-164.

120    http://s3.amazonaws.com/illustrativemathematics/illustration_pdfs/000/000/806/original/illustrative_mathematics_806.pdf?1390749189 (Accessed 24 May 2014).

121    Journal, Diary, What's the Difference?: http://quinncreative.wordpress.com/2007/08/26/journal-diary-whats-the-difference/ (Accessed 24 May 2014); Difference between Journal and Diary: http://www.differencebetween.com/difference-between-journal-and-vs-diary/ (Accessed 24 May 2014).

122    Since there are countless video sources that discuss and explore the lives of African Americans during the Civil War, these are just suggestions: *Black History: A Retrospective*. DVD. Directed by Various. (Golden Valley, MN: Mill Creek Entertainment, 2010). http://www.amazon.com/Black-History-Retrospective-Barack-Obama/dp/B002WBYDLC (Accessed 24 May 2014); *African Americans: Many Rivers to Cross*. DVD. Directed by Phil Bertelsen, Leslie Asko Gladsjo, Sabrin Streeter, Jamilla Wignot. (Arlington, VA: Kunhardt McGee Productions & Inkwell Films, PBS, 2014). http://www.pbs.org/wnet/african-americans-many-rivers-to-cross/ (Accessed 24 May 2014).

123    Originally developed in 1956, Bloom's Taxonomy, is a classification of levels of intellectual behavior in learning. The goal is for teachers to slowly work their students up the levels from Knowledge (basic memorization) to Comprehension (or understanding) to Application (actively applying what they have learned) to Analysis (or deconstruction) to Synthesis (infusing new information with prior knowledge) and finally to Evaluation (a critical examination of new material). It was later updated and revised by a group of cognitive psychologists during the 1900s and currently begins with Remembering (or recalling information) to Understanding (or explaining) to Applying (in a new way) to Analyzing (distinguishing between different parts) to Evaluation (justifying their decisions) to Creating (actively creating new knowledge). http://ww2.odu.edu/educ/roverbau/Bloom/blooms_taxonomy.htm (Accessed 24 May 2014).

124    African American Civil War Timeline, http://www.pbs.org/wgbh/americanexperience/features/timeline/lincolns-soldiers/ (Accessed 24 May 2014); The History Place: A Nation Divided (The U.S. Civil War 1861-1865), http://www.historyplace.com/civilwar/ (Accessed 24 May 2014).

125    One suggested weekly blog can be found at www.kayewisewhitehead.com, (Ac-

cessed 24 May 2014).

126    The document is available at the National Archives website http://www.archives. gov/exhibits/featured_documents/emancipation_proclamation/transcript.html (Accessed 24 May 2014).

127    Two brief and differing perspectives are offered by historians by John Hope Franklin, "The Emancipation Proclamation: An Act of Justice," Prologue Magazine, Summer 1993, Volume 25, No. 2. http://www.archives.gov/publications/prologue/1993/summer/emancipation-proclamation.html (Accessed 24 May 2014); Paul Finkelman's "Disunion: Lincoln's Letter to the Editor," The Opinion Pages, New York Times, August 23, 2012.

128    Newspaper articles are available at the Library of Congress Website, "Chronicling America Historic American Newspapers" http://chroniclingamerica.loc.gov (Accessed 24 May 2014)

129    See Orville Vernon Burton and James McPherson, "Burton & McPherson on Abe Lincoln's Leadership Style" http://www.britannica.com/EBchecked/media/140883/Historians-O-Vernon-Burton-and-James-McPherson-commenting-on-how (Accessed 24 May 2014).

130    Letter from Frederick Douglass to Major George L. Stearns, August 1863 http://www.gilderlehrman.org/sites/all/themes/gli/panels/civilwar150/Douglass_Letter_to_Stearns.pdf (Accessed 24 May 2014); Letter from Abraham Lincoln General Nathaniel P. Banks (Louisiana) on Reconstruction, August 5, 1863. http://teachingamericanhistory.org/library/document/letter-to-general-n-p-banks/ (Accessed 24 May 2014).
Letter from Abraham Lincoln to James C. Conkling on Emancipation, August 26, 1863 http://www.abrahamlincolnonline.org/lincoln/speeches/conkling.htm (Accessed 24 May 2014); Horace Greeley, "A Prayer for Twenty Millions," New York Tribune, August 20, 1862. http://faculty.assumption.edu/aas/Manuscripts/greeley.html (Accessed 24 May 2014).

131    See Theodore Hershberg's "Free Blacks in Antebellum Philadelphia: A Study of Ex-Slaves, Freeborn, and Socioeconomic Decline" in *African Americans in Pennsylvania: Shifting Historical Perspectives*. Edited by Joe William Trotter, Jr. and Eric Ledell Smith. (University Park: The Pennsylvania State University Press, 1997) or see Gerald G. Eggert's "'Two Steps Forward a Step and a Half Back': Harrisburg's African American Community in the Nineteenth Century." Ibid.

132    If necessary, call attention to Daniel Sutherland's observation that Northern wartime demands resulted in more than 300,000 women, many of them from rural districts, joining the urban industrial work force. This demographic shift forever changed the face of American industry and everyday life. In The Expansion of Everyday Life 1860 – 1876, Sutherland noted that, "What began as a wartime emergency became a permanent revolution… Women who operated their own shops often enjoyed quite respectable positions." Ibid, 165.

133    *Notes from a Colored Girl*, 159-172.

134    Catherine Clinton, *The Other Civil War: American Women in the Nineteenth Century* (New York: Hill and Wang, 1984), 21-39.

135    Sample questions could include: What were to be the limits of democratic control in the United States? If all labor, black as well as white, became free and were given schools and the right to vote, what control could or should be set to the power and action of these laborers? Du Bois, *Black Reconstruction in America*, 13.

136    Joyce Appleby, Lynn Hunt, and Margaret Jacob, *Telling the Truth About History*

(New York: W. W. Norton & Company, 1994), 55.

137    See the Library of Congress' website: "Chronicling America, Historic American Newspapers" http://chroniclingamerica.loc.gov or Cornell University and the University of Michigan's "Making of America." http://quod.lib.umich.edu/m/moagrp/ (Accessed 24 May 2014); Time permitting, students can examine The Ladies' Repository, a monthly periodical, devoted to literature, arts, and religion in order to familiarize themselves visually to the fashion trends of middle and upper-class women from the period, which may be found on the "Making of America" database.

138    For more on Emilie's religious practices, see Chapter 2 from *Notes from a Colored Girl*, 62-85.

139    Ibid, 2.

140    http://chroniclingamerica.loc.gov/lccn/sn83025925/ ; http://chroniclingamerica.loc.gov/lccn/sn83032300/ (Accessed 24 May 2014).

141    Any section of text may be used; however, Du Bois's chapters on "The Black Worker" or "The White Worker" are particularly appropriate for the week's lesson. See Du Bois, *Black Reconstruction in America*, 17-22.

142    http://valley.lib.virginia.edu (Accessed 24 May 2014).

143    http://ocp.hul.harvard.edu/ww/records.html (Accessed 24 May 2014).

Apprentice House is the country's only campus-based, student-staffed book publishing company. Directed by professors and industry professionals, it is a nonprofit activity of the Communication Department at Loyola University Maryland.

Using state-of-the-art technology and an experiential learning model of education, Apprentice House publishes books in untraditional ways. This dual responsibility as publishers and educators creates an unprecedented collaborative environment among faculty and students, while teaching tomorrow's editors, designers, and marketers.

Outside of class, progress on book projects is carried forth by the AH Book Publishing Club, a co-curricular campus organization supported by Loyola University Maryland's Office of Student Activities.

Eclectic and provocative, Apprentice House titles intend to entertain as well as spark dialogue on a variety of topics. Financial contributions to sustain the press's work are welcomed. Contributions are tax deductible to the fullest extent allowed by the IRS.

To learn more about Apprentice House books or to obtain submission guidelines, please visit www.apprenticehouse.com.

Apprentice House
Communication Department
Loyola University Maryland
4501 N. Charles Street
Baltimore, MD 21210
Ph: 410-617-5265 • Fax: 410-617-2198
info@apprenticehouse.com • www.apprenticehouse.com